ENGLISH WEATHERVANES

NORTH EAST

WEST SOUTH

THE 'LION VANE'
OF
MAXSTOKE CASTLE.

ENGLISH WEATHERVANES

THEIR STORIES AND LEGENDS
FROM
MEDIEVAL TO MODERN TIMES

By

A. NEEDHAM, F.R.S.A., A.M.C.
(Author of " How to Study an Old Church ")

WITH 275 DRAWINGS BY THE AUTHOR

CHARLES CLARKE LIMITED
HAYWARDS HEATH, SUSSEX

First Published 1953

Printed and Published by

CHARLES CLARKE (HAYWARDS HEATH) LIMITED
12/13 BOLTRO ROAD · HAYWARDS HEATH · SUSSEX

CONTENTS

The above drawing is a design by the author for a
weathervane on the gable of a children's orphanage

ENGLISH WEATHERVANES

THEIR STORIES AND LEGENDS
FROM
MEDIEVAL TO MODERN TIMES

PREFACE

In the large number of books dealing with architecture, weather-vanes, in some cases designed by the architect of the building to surmount a spire, tower, cupola, pinnacle, etc., and serve as decorative features in addition to their functional purpose, are not even mentioned ; yet many of these objects are beautiful examples of craftsmanship both in design and execution.

Weathervanes provide an open-air museum of the wrought-iron work of blacksmiths. Even where, in some cases, copper forms part of the vane, blacksmiths, famed for their versatility, would not hesitate to use this metal. So many people merely associate these men in their minds with the shoeing of horses, but these fine crafts-men have, through many centuries, also executed beautiful examples of metal objects for churches, mansions, farms, etc. Few members of the public bestow upon weathervanes the attention they deserve, thus losing much of interest which would add enjoyment to their walks and excursions.

This book has been compiled as an introduction to the study of English weathervanes. The drawings have been made from weathervanes seen in several counties and, although the total area of the country covered in the search for examples was comparatively small, more than 300 (237 are included in this book) were discovered, which indicates how numerous and varied in design they are on our town and country buildings. Many weathervanes have similar subjects for their designs, but it is interesting to note how they vary in treatment so that rarely are two exactly alike to be found. In this book 21 weathercocks and 18 " ship " vanes are illustrated, yet all differ from one another. It is possible to see duplicates of a few modern weathervanes such as those on Plate 25, Fig. 63

and Plate 36, Figs. 68 and 72, which are made by firms who stock a few set designs for those clients having no individual ideas of their own.

The term weathervane is a misleading one. One day, in Littlehampton, Sussex, a small boy sidled up to me and asked what I was doing. I drew his attention to a nearby weathervane which I was sketching. He thought for a moment or two and then said, '' Weathervane ! Will it be fine for our ' outing ' to-morrow ? '' I was obliged to explain that weathervanes merely show the direction the wind is blowing from, and that this was only one of the many things that had to be considered before one could forecast the weather.

The above incident certainly indicates that wind-vane, the word used in the *Meteorological Observers' Handbook*, issued by the Air Ministry (Meteorological Office), is a better term. However, as they are so commonly called weathercocks and weathervanes I shall use these terms in this book.

During journeys for the purpose of making drawings of the weathervanes illustrated in this book, obtaining owners' permission to sketch them, and in seeking information about them, I have aroused much interest with my requests. Several owners, whose vanes were in poor condition, had them restored shortly after my visit.

Not the least interesting part of my search for weathervanes has been the contacts made with blacksmiths, who, with a few tools similar to those used by smiths for many centuries, are still turning out excellent wrought-iron work in the way of weathervanes, gates, screens, signs, etc. I noted the pleasure these men derive from a piece of hand-work well done. It is stimulating to learn that there are members of the public who encourage these craftsmen and do not object to paying for good hand-wrought metal work. The Rural Industries Bureau is also doing much to help country craftsmen.

I have found it convenient to group the weathervanes illustrated in this book into four sections : those on churches, public buildings, business premises and private dwellings, for in some instances the vanes have designs signifying their connection with the buildings or the tenants.

Some weathervanes have interesting stories and legends connected with them, and brief notes accompany each drawing in this book. Details such as dates of erection, whether the existing vane was the original one, names of the makers of the vanes, etc., were often difficult to obtain. Many church and public buildings records contain no reference to the weathervane on the building. Records

6

of " Old " St. Paul's Cathedral, London, which was commenced in 1087, reveal that the weathercock on the spire was renewed several times before the building was destroyed by the Great Fire in 1666.

The drawings of the majority of the illustrations in this book have been made possible by the invaluable assistance of my wife, acting as " spotter," as I drove my car around the countryside.

I wish also to acknowledge the help so readily given me by the following :—

Director of the Air Ministry (Meteorological Office) ; the Assistant Astronomer (Greenwich Observatory) ; the Keeper of the British Museum ; the Director of the Victoria and Albert Museum ; the Librarians of the Royal Institute of British Architects, the Royal Society of Arts, the Andover Public and the East Sussex County ; the Town Clerk of Bradford-on-Avon ; the Publicity Officer of British Railways ; the Secretary of the Leathersellers' Company ; the Secretary of the Rugby Football Union, and the Automobile Association. Miss A. Baker and Mr. W. G. Busbridge of the " Friends of Abingdon Society," Mrs. A. Mee, the Misses F. Bassett-Freestone, M. Gambell and M. McNair ; the Reverends Andrew Gray, T. C. Jones, P. J. F. Simpson and J. H. Unwin ; Messrs. S. W. Broadbent, G. Chapman, A. S. Downing, S. Everson, C. Farthing, J. T. Fetherston-Dilke (Lieut., R.N.), W. R. Gillett, A. E. Graves, R. E. Kerley, F. J. Martin, J. F. Nichols, F.S.A., V. C. Osborne and J. E. Taylor, M.A., and other friends who have reported the location of interesting weathervanes, provided information about them, and owners of weathervanes who gave me permission to sketch them.

The dimensions of weathervanes are often deceptive. Large vanes on very tall steeples may appear less in size than smaller ones on low buildings.

If this book succeeds in influencing members of the public to appreciate these examples of craftsmanship, and persuades those who have good weathervanes on their buildings to preserve them in these days when the use of machines and mass-production methods tend to limit the output of good hand-wrought work, it will serve a useful purpose.

A.N.

A Brief History of English Weathervanes

A definition, printed in the *Encyclopaedia Britannica*, gives no indication of the extremely interesting examples of craftwork in iron and copper that are revealed by the study of English weathervanes.

" Vane (formerly spelt ' fane,' i.e., pennon, flag) ; c.f. Ger., Fahne ; Du., Vaan ; Fr., Girouette ; Ital., Banderuola ; Ger., Wetterfahne (the weathercock on a steeple).   Vanes seem in early times to have been of various forms as dragons, &c. ; but in the Tudor period the favourite design was a beast or bird sitting on a slender pedestal and carrying an upright rod, on which a thin plate of metal is hung like a flag, ornamented in various ways," see Fig 7, Plate XXVI.

The origin of weathervanes is lost in the dim past.   It may be that smoke first drew primitive man's attention to the changing direction of the wind.   When he lit a fire at the mouth of his cave to protect his family from the attacks of wild beasts he would notice that, on some days, his dwelling would be unpleasantly filled with smoke, while at other times the smoke drifted away from the cave. Then he would come to learn, when hunting animals for food and clothing, that it was necessary to approach his prey from the windward side so that the animal should not pick up his scent and thus be on the alert.

During the time the Romans occupied Britain they used smoke for signalling in the daytime (e.g., from the Roman lighthouse at Dover) and from the forts of the Saxon shore, and the smoke would serve equally to indicate the direction of the wind.

Small flags, blown in various directions by changing winds may have suggested the making and use of weathervanes.   Evidence of the very early use of flags exists, a few examples are given below, with drawings on Plate I.   As will be seen from the illustrations in this book, weathervanes have, for centuries, been made in flag-like shapes.

Carvings and paintings, supplemented by ancient writings, show that companies of the Egyptian army carried staves having such emblems as sacred animals, boats, figures, etc., representing " Nomes " or districts   These staves were frequently ornamented below the emblem with streamers.   Fig. 1, Plate I, is an illustration of one such staff from a bas-relief on the Abydos Temple of Seti I

(c. 1300 B.C., XIXth Dynasty). When the bearers carried these staves, with the streamers flowing in the wind, the archers discharging their arrows, and having to take into consideration the direction and velocity of the wind would, no doubt, find the streamers of use as indicators.

Part of the facade of the temple of Luxor (restored by Ch. Chipiez), shows, in Fig. 2, Plate I, a pole with streamers serving as decoration, which could also play their part as wind direction indicators. The temple was begun under Amenhotep III, c. 1400 B.C.

Fig. 5, Plate I, shows the spear, with small flag attached, carried by Grecian soldiers as depicted on the famous " Warrior Vase " (Mycenæan Age in Greece, 1600-1100 B.C.). It may be the origin of the pennons on the lances of Medieval knights.

The drawing (from a restoration after Thiersch) in Fig. 3, Plate I, shows the upper part of the ancient Pharos (lighthouse), built under Ptolemy II, about 260 B.C., and accounted one of the seven wonders of the world. It stood on the island of Pharos at the entrance to the harbour of Alexandria. It appears to have two long streamers which would show mariners the direction of the wind.

Livy (59 B.C.-A.D. 17) describes the Vexillum, the standard of the cavalry of the ancient Roman army, as a square piece of cloth fastened to a piece of wood fixed crosswise at the end of a spear.

A reconstruction of the Circus Maximus (4th century) shows tall poles having streamers attached to them, see Fig. 12, Plate I.

Illustrations of ships in the years B.C. do not indicate that flags were used on them, but Fig. 10, Plate I, a drawing from a Bœotian fibula, made of bronze, and now in the British Museum, shows a Greek boat (about 8th century) which carries a banner-like flag at the top of the mast, so that it is possible that flags on ships were used in earlier years.

Figs. 6, 8 and 9, Plate I, illustrate pennons on the lances of knights of the 11th century as seen on the Bayeux Tapestry. A banner on the lance of Simon de Montfort, c. 1231, is shown in Fig. 15, Plate I, while in Fig. 6, is the pennon on the lance of St. John D'Abernon, 1277, shown on the " brass " in Stoke D'Abernon Church, Surrey, stated to be the earliest specimen of a " brass " in England.

That the suggestions as to the origin of weathervanes mentioned earlier, are not unreasonable, is indicated by the statement in the recent issue of the Air Ministry's *Meteorological Observers' Handbook*, to the effect that, in the absence of a vane, a good wind indicator is furnished by a streamer (a long narrow flag) attached to a tall flag-staff in an open situation ; and the direction of smoke should be noted also.

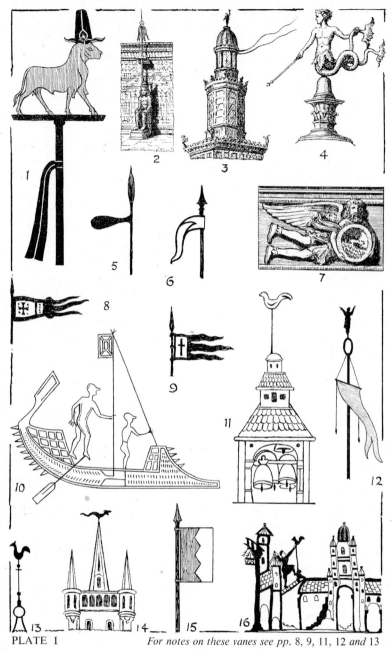

1   2   3   4

5   6   7

8   9

10   11   12

13   14   15   16

PLATE I   *For notes on these vanes see pp.* 8, 9, 11, 12 *and* 13

10

Whatever it was that suggested the making and erecting of weathervanes, they have been, and still continue to be, most useful to mankind. Even in these times when, through the British Broadcasting service, weather reports are regularly sent out, they are general ones covering wide areas, and local winds may vary in direction, which would be shown by the vanes on nearby buildings.

Vitruvius, *De Architectura*, Lib. I.C.ij, refers to what may have been the earliest weathervane, surmounting " The Horologion," of Andronicus Cyrrhestes (the so-called " Tower of the Winds " in Athens), c. 50 B.C.

A translation reads : ". . . they put also a golden Triton holding a rod in its right hand and it is constructed in such a way that it is turned by the wind in such a manner that it always stays against the wind, holding the rod as an indication above the image of the blowing wind." Fig. 4, Plate I, is from a reconstruction of the Triton on top of the tower, by J. C. Basing, sculptor ; for the vane is now missing. (Note.—Triton. In Greek mythology, a minor sea diety, son of Poseidon, represented as part man, part fish).

The " Tower of Winds " is an octagonal building with a frieze representing the eight winds (N., N.E., E., S.E., S., S.W., W., N.W.). One of these figures, " Kaikias " (shield full of hail), signifying the north east wind is shown in Fig. 7, Plate I. (Radcliffe Observatory, built at Oxford in the 18th century, has a tower based on the " Tower of Winds," and having the eight sculptured figures representing the winds).

There is little indication of other very early weathervanes except, it is reported that Rome had a somewhat similar building to the " Tower of Winds," and that in the 4th century a female figure turned in the wind over a building in Constantinople. An illustration in the *History of Skylitzes* (from Schlumberger, *L'épopée byzantine*, Hachette), depicts the East Roman Empress Zoe (who died A.D. 1050), leaving the church of S. Sophia, Constantinople, and entering her Palace. On the church is shown a weathercock with a cross above it. The cock, like all other Christian symbols, was probably eliminated by the Turks when they converted the church into a mosque in 1543, or it may only have existed in the artist's imagination. In spite of the paucity of evidence it must not be assumed that other vanes were not in use during this early period. It may be possible that the Romans, during their occupation of Britain, used weathervanes here.

If one peruses the many literary references in the past, it can be appreciated that weathervanes were considered of much interest and importance. A few of these notes are given in the following extracts, with dates and translations where necessary.

R. K. Gordon in *Anglo-Saxon Poetry*, gives a quaint 8th century description (an Old English idea of a riddle), the answer in this case being a '' weathercock.''

'' I am puff-breasted, swollen necked. I have a head and lofty tail, eyes and ears and one foot, a back and hard beak, a high neck and two sides, a rod in the middle, a dwelling above man, I endure misery when he who stirs the forest moves me, and torrents beat upon me in my station, the hard hail and rime ; and frost comes down and snow falls on me pierced through the stomach and I . . .'' (Description is incomplete). Note : Shakespeare makes *King Lear* (Act III, Scene II) defiantly exclaim :

'' Blow, winds, and crack your cheeks ! rage ! blow !
Your cataracts and hurricanoes, spout
Till you have drenched our steeples, drown'd the cocks !

A contemporary drawing in the 10th century *Benedictional of St. Ethelwold*, shows the weathercock on the tower of Winchester Cathedral, see Fig. 11, Plate I.

A part of the Bayeux Tapestry, which is over 800 years old, shows a man, with a weathercock in his hand, about to mount the roof of Westminster Abbey (dedicated to St. Peter), built during the time of Edward the Confessor, and consecrated in 1065. Fig. 16, Plate I, shows the portion of the Tapestry referred to.

Memorials of Canterbury Cathedral, by C. E. Woodruff and W. Danks, contains a reference to the '' guilded seraph on the top of Canterbury Cathedral.'' This was probably a weathervane. No date is given, but a 12th century drawing shows, over the west end turrets of Canterbury Cathedral, two weathercocks.

c. 1233. Fig. 13, Plate I, is a copy of part of an engraving depicting a weathercock on the tower of a hospital at Oxford, built by Henry III (MS. Roy, 14c, vii).

In the 13th century a royal licence was required for the use of weathervanes, and these were restricted to the nobility. Small pennons were attached to the head of the lance and borne by a knight, sometimes having his cognizance upon it ; see Figs. 6, 8 and 9, Plate I. It was usual in battle, to grant to the first knight to plant his pennon on the walls of a besieged town or castle, the Royal right to fix upon the highest part of his own castle or stronghold, his vane, emblazoned with his bearing or crest. Probably the primary object of these vanes was to display the arms of the knight ; showing the direction of the wind being of secondary importance.

c. 1300 Neckham. *De Utensilibus* (i.e., about utensils), quoted in Wright's *Old English Vocabularies*, has a reference to a weathercock : '' Ventilogium, Veder-coc.''

c. 1307. In the *Cottonian MS Nero* D II, in the British Museum, a large weathercock is shown on the spire of St. Paul's Cathedral.

c. 1340. *The Ayen-bite of Inwit* (The Again-bite of the Inner Knowledge), by Richard Rolle, of Hampole, contains some words, the approximate translation being : " Therefore they beeth as the weathercock that is upon the steeple, that himself turns with each wind."

1365. In *Exch. K.R. Accts.* 462, 23 is stated that, in A.D. 1365, a weathervane was set up on the great tower of Dover Castle which was helpful to navigators of ships.

c. 1400. " Against women unconstant " is the title of a balade —a short poem of three seven-lined stanzas, ascribed to Chaucer, which includes the following : " But, as a wedercok that turneth his face with every wind, ye fare, and that is sene."

c. 1425. *Parochial Antiquities*, Vol. II, Kennet. " With two wind-readers, namely vanes of tin bought ———— to be put on each end of the said dormitory." (i.e., on the gables).

1479-1481. From the records of St. Mary-at-Hill Church, London. " Item for mendyng of the vane of the steple."

c. 1480. " Testament of Cresseid," a poem by Robert Henryson, a Scottish poet. The poem is a sequel to Chaucer's " Troilus and Cressida." (Note.—It is called a Testament because it contains her dying speech at the end). The part relating to a weathercock reads :—

> " Thairfoir I reidze tak a ze find,
>   For they are sad as weddercock in wind."
> (15th century Scottish dialect).

An approximate translation is :—
> " Therefore I advise ye take them as ye find,
>   For they are as fixed as a weathercock in the wind."

c. 1483. A quotation from Caxton. " Be not like ne semblable the tortuse ne the crane which wynde their hede here and there as a vane." (Note.—"ne," i.e., nor).

In Henry the Seventh's time, a poet in *Tower of Doctrine* gives the following :—
> " The little turrets with ymages of golde about was set, which with the wynde aye moved."

Fig. 14, Plate I, shows part of a building in an illustration from *Artillery in Action*, temp. Henry VIII, from an English treatise on artillery ; MS. Cott. Vesp. A. xvii (British Museum). On top of the building is a weathervane which appears to be in the form of some kind of dragon.

c. 1515.   *Archaeologia X*, 85, contains an account of the erection of a weathercock on Louth church steeple in the presence of priests who sang the Te Deum Laudamus.   Afterwards the bells were rung, and bread and ale was distributed to the people.

c. 1546.   *Church Goods (in the Diocese of) York* (a publication of the Surtees Society).   '' The said steple havyng a whether cokke thereuppon all gylt.''

c. 1548.   Hall.   *Chronicles of Henry VIII.*   '' Over the gates wer arches with towers embattailed, set with vanes and scutchions of the armes of the Emperor and the Kyng.''

1597.   In *The Wisdom of Solomon Paraphrased*, by T. Middleton, is the following :—'' Like a vane turn'd with every blast.''

1606.   A record in the Spalding Club, Aberdeen Burgh, reads : —'' 16th April, 1606.   David Anderstone, maister of Kirk wark to send brazen cok of the stepill of Sanct Nicolas Parish Kirk this burght of Flanderis to be medit thair and owergilt and to be erectit and set vp vpon the hicht of the said stepill.''

1661.   In the records of All Saints' Church, Hereford, 1661. '' To John Williams, plasterer, for pulling downe and putting up the whether cocke.''   (This probably refers to doing the necessary repairs, or perhaps to the periodical cleaning of the bearing to ensure that the weathercock turned in the wind).

1662.   The Vicar of Bray, mentioned by Thomas Fuller in his *History of the Worthies of England*, was likened to a weathercock because of his frequent change of opinions.

The celebrated Vicar lived in the reigns of Henry VIII, Edward VI, Queen Mary and Queen Elizabeth.   In order to retain his Office he was, in turn, a Papist, then a Protestant, and again a Papist and afterwards a Protestant.

Part of the well-known song about the Vicar reads :—
> '' For this is law I will maintain
> Until my dying day, Sir,
> That whatsoever King doth reign
> I'll be the Vicar of Bray, Sir.''

1683.   D.A. in *Art of Converse*.   '' Some are as changeable as weathercocks in their humours.''

1833.   L. Ritchie.   *Wand Loire*.   '' The Duc de Choiseul—— consoled himself by setting up the head of Voltaire as a weathercock.''

1864.   '' Aylmer's Field,'' a poem by Tennyson, includes the following :—'' Whose blazing wyvern weathercocked the spire.''

1867.   H. Latham.   *Black and White*.   '' The most conspicuous weathercock in the town is a golden trumpet on the spire of one of the churches.''

Many more literary references to weathervanes could be quoted.

Figs. 2 and 5, Plate IV, show what are reputed to be the oldest English weathercock and weathervane still in use.

A number of vanes have, as part of their design, the date when they were made ; but it must not be assumed that these vanes are, in every case, the original ones. Evidence shows, that some having been blown down and broken, copies of the original vanes were made and erected in the place of the damaged one.

Early weathervanes in this country were of a banner-like form without a pointer, see Fig. 5, Plate IV, and Figs. 6 and 7, Plate XXVI. It is not possible to state when pointers first came into general use. A vane, dated 1577, see Fig. 1, Plate XXVI, is shown with a pointer, as are some 17th century ones, see Plates IV, V and XI.

Good examples of vanes, which might otherwise have been lost when buildings were pulled down, have been saved by some museum authorities (including the Victoria and Albert, London), who thought the vanes were worth preserving and exhibiting, see Figs. 2 and 6, Plate XI, Figs. 13 and 14, Plate XII, and Fig. 7, Plate XVI.

Lighthouse keepers, having to write weather records, are provided with weathervanes fitted with interior dials, somewhat similar to the Greenwich Observatory one, see Plate II.

Few people realise that there are still in position, in some parts of this country, very old telegraph poles with weathervanes on top of them, see Fig. 16, Plate XIII.

There are other vanes, which, while they cannot strictly be termed weathervanes, are operated by the wind, and are so constructed that they turn the objects they are fixed upon until they are in the most favourable position for their purpose, see Plate XIX, Figs. 21, 22, 26, 27, 28, and Plate XXXVII, Fig. 79.

Some modern weathervane designs in the form of representations of human figures, animals, etc., can be seen painted in naturalistic colours which rarely add to their artistic appearance, and, unless the vanes are on a low building, the colour is not easily seen. There are, however, cases in which colour is an advantage, such as those depicting dalmatian dogs, see Plate XXIII, Fig. 51, or when a design shows a special breed of cow and colour would make it easier to identify the breed.

That the colouring of weathervanes is not a modern innovation can be seen by the following extract :—*Select. Rec. Oxford* (W. H. Turner). '' For . . . coloring the beasts and the vanes and the Quenes arms . . . with colors and oyles.''

Sir W. St. J. Hope in *Windsor Castle*, A.D. 1352, refers to a vane on the Hall at Windsor which was painted with the King's Arms.

Gilded weathervanes have a very picturesque appearance, showing flashes of bright gold against a blue sky as they turn in the wind. This aspect is referred to by Scott, in *Woodstock*, Vol. II (A.D. 1826), " One or two . . . venerable turrets, bearing each its own vane of rare device glittering in the sun,'' and also by L. Morris, in *Ode of Life* (A.D. 1880), " The old grey church, with the tall spire, whose vane the sun sets fire.''

Weathervanes constructed of copper turn a lovely green colour which is enhanced when the sun shines on them. This colour, when copper is exposed to the atmosphere, is caused by the formation of basic copper carbonate from the reaction of the copper, moisture and carbon di-oxide. The colour varies, due to environment ; in town air, copper sulphate is a constituent, while by the sea, copper sulphide is produced.

This brief survey is sufficient to indicate that the use of weathervanes in this country has continued for many centuries, and their use shows little sign of waning popularity.

Recording Weathervanes

The photographing of weathervanes, even with a telephoto lens, is not easy, and often produces an unsatisfactory result. Weathervanes consist of two parts ; the moveable vane, and the fixed shaft with arms and letters indicating the cardinal points. For a correct picture, the moveable vane should be parallel to the face of the film in the camera, and the arms, with letters and any iron scroll work in such a position as to display the design to the best advantage. Such a view, particularly on a windy day, is difficult to secure.

A sketch book, pencil and a pair of binoculars are the best things to use when making a pictorial record of weathervanes. Armed with these, it is possible to draw the fixed part of the vane from one point of view, and the moveable part from another position if necessary.

When viewed from a distance, the majority of weathervanes appear against the light sky as pictorial silhouettes. Most people are familiar with the silhouettes or " shadow " portraits and pictures which were popular before the invention of photography, and are still executed in small numbers. For these silhouettes, a person was so placed that a light cast the shadow of his or her profile on a screen, and a reproduction of the shadow, life size, or smaller, was cut by scissors from black paper and stuck on a light background, or painted in black on ivory card, silk, vellum, porcelain and glass. Fig. A below shows part of an 18th century silhouette picture. It

A

is possible that some of the designers of weathervanes similar to those shown in Fig. 37, Plate XV ; Fig. 24, Plate XIX ; Fig. 19, Plate XXVIII ; Fig. 37, Plate XXX ; Fig. 38, Plate XXXI; Figs. 57 and 61, Plate XXXIV; Figs. 72 and 73, Plate XXXVI ; and others depicted in this book, may have been influenced by the old silhouette pictures.

This silhouette appearance is used for the illustrations of the weathervanes in this book, with the exception of those built up in more or less rounded shapes, when the effects of light and shade created by their varying forms are indicated.

The wrought-iron scroll work, supporting the four arms, with letters indicating the cardinal points is, in some cases, very elaborate. To display the design of this scroll work clearly some drawings show only two for the four arms. In other cases it has been possible to draw the four arms when this view creates an impression of a beautiful filigree effect of wrought-iron scrolls and curves.

It has been necessary to group several drawings on each page, and, as the size of the objects depicted varied considerably, it was not always possible to draw them all to the same scale.

Construction, Erection and Use
of Weathervanes

As the use of aeroplanes becomes more prevalent, the need for accurate weather reports assumes greater importance, and so more and more specially equipped weather-stations are being set up on land and sea in an increasing number of places in the world. Members of the stations who study weather conditions and issue reports naturally require weathervanes, which form part of their equipment, to be constructed and erected in an efficient manner.

The drawings on Plate II illustrate the weathervane (which has been in use for 100 years) on the Royal Observatory, at Greenwich. "A" in Fig. I is an elevation of the moveable vane which records the direction of the wind on a dial, while "B" and "C" is an apparatus, situated two feet below the vane (part "C" being a circular pressure plate), moving with the vane; wind pressure causes the circular plate to compress springs and the movements are registered on another dial. The dials are housed in a turret, the upper part of which is shown in Fig. I, while the dials are depicted in Figs. 2, 4 and 5.

In addition to the dials, recordings are made with a carbon pencil on paper by means of the apparatus shown as elevation and plan in Figs. 2 and 3. "E" is the spindle from the vane, "D" and "F" the dials, "G" a toothed wheel operating the toothed edge of a moveable bar "H" which is supported by roller guides "J," fixed to the table "L." Fig. 3 is a plan of the bar, supports, wheel and carbon pencil holder "K."

On Plate III, Fig. 3 illustrates the design of a wind-vane, recommended by the Air Ministry (in the *Meteorological Observers' Handbook*), to be constructed of copper. When used on aerodrome buildings a dial is painted on the ceiling and a pointer fixed to the spindle of the vane so that interior readings can be made. The end of a vane opposite to the pointer has the larger surface area of metal for the wind to exert pressure on and thus turn the vane. The small diagram in Fig. 3 represents a view looking down on a vane, to show the action of the wind. "B" is the spindle on which the vane turns, "A" the pointer end, and "C" the larger surface area of the vane. The wind blows in the direction of the arrows "E," thus, as "C" has a larger surface area than "A" the wind would exert more pressure on this end, moving the vane in the

19

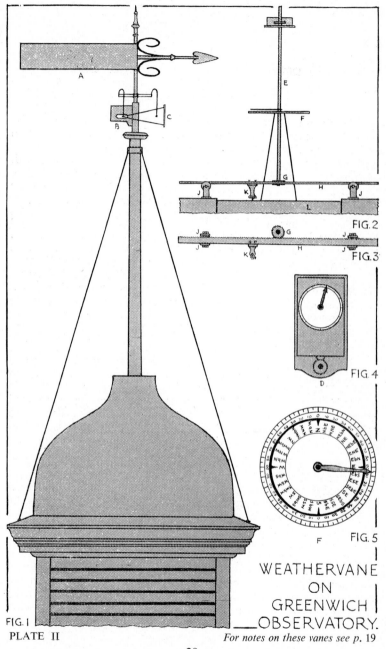

A

C

B

E

F

G

J   K   H   J

L

FIG. 2

J   G   J

K   H   H   FIG. 3

D

FIG. 4

F   FIG. 5

WEATHERVANE
ON
GREENWICH
OBSERVATORY.

FIG. 1
PLATE II

For notes on these vanes see p. 19

20

direction shown by the arrow " F," until, when it reaches the position shown by the dotted lines, it is end on to the wind, and would remain in this position until the direction of the wind changes.

Another type of wind-vane used on aerodromes is the one shown in Fig. 2, known as a " sleeve." It consists of a hollow canvas cone-like shape on a ring and short rod attached to a bearing on a tall pole. The wind, blowing through the cone, swings it round until the rod points to the quarter the wind is blowing from.

While the majority of weathervanes act as described above, there are some, built up in the form of models of ships, complete with sails, which are constructed so that they move like a ship running before the wind ; thus the stern of the vessel faces the direction from which the wind is blowing, see Fig. 17, Plate XIII and Fig. 36, Plate XV.

On Plate III a form of wind-vane, known as an anemometer, used to measure the velocity of the wind, is shown in Fig. 1. This apparatus consists of three or four arms ; at the end of each is a hemispherical cup. The junction of the arms is attached to a vertical spindle, the lower end of which is connected to cog-wheels, arranged to count the rotation of the arms, and translate this into miles per hour, recording the result on a dial. When the anemometer is erected some distance from the building used by the observer, it is fitted up to make an electrical recording.

A weathervane must be able to move easily, and so the form of bearing employed is important, and it should be examined periodically and cleaned if it is corroded. Six varieties of bearings, shown in section, are illustrated by Figs. 6 to 11 inclusive on Plate III. Parts in solid black are the fixed portions of the bearings, while the moveable parts are shown by shaded lines drawn at an angle. A small clearance is arranged between fixed and moving parts to allow for expansion of the metal. The vane is brazed or bolted to the moveable part of the bearing. In Fig. 6 the tapered end of the rod revolves on a glass marble in a metal disc. The end of the rod in Fig. 7 is in a tapered hole in a bronze disc. A similar bearing is shown in Fig. 10, but in this case the rod is fixed and the tube turns. In Fig. 8 both the fixed and moveable ends have a concave recess and a steel ball allows for free movement. The bearing shown in Fig. 9 shows the form used for the vane illustrated by Fig. 3, and consists of a small metal rod revolving in a cylindrical recess in the fixed rod. Fig. 11 illustrates an ordinary ball-bearing, the outer part fixed in the tube, while the inner part has a rod (tightly fixed into it), so that the rod can revolve with the inner part of the bearing. At the lower end of the rod is a brass collar to keep the rod vertical. The splayed ends of the rods or tubes are so made to prevent water entering the bearing and causing rust and corrosion.

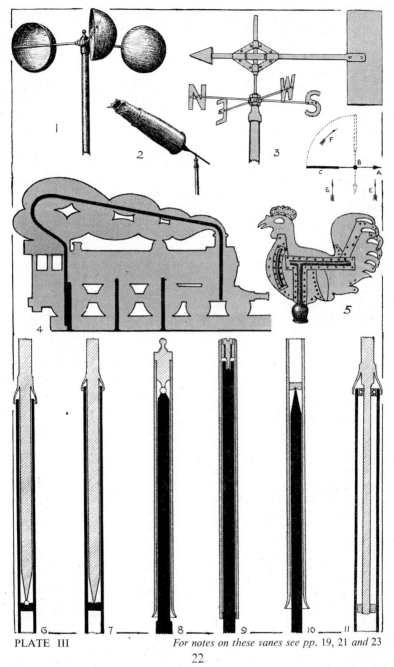

PLATE III

For notes on these vanes see pp. 19, 21 *and* 23

22

It will be noticed that one half of a weathervane has a larger surface of metal than the pointer end which, therefore, must be weighted to create a correct blance. The arrow head of the vane, Fig. 3, is a thick piece of lead. The pointer end of the large weathervane at the Rugby Union's ground at Twickenham, see Fig. 29, Plate XIV, has a weight equal to 60lb. to afford the correct balance.

Weathervanes having a large area of sheet metal would bend in strong winds, so metal rods are used to strengthen them. Figs. 4 and 5, Plate III, show these rods on the " engine " (see Plate XIII, Fig. 20), and the " cock " which has surmounted the spire of Norwich Cathedral since 1660, having been repaired on occasions. A story is told of a sailor who was " dared " to climb this spire, but it is not recorded whether he made good his boast to sit astride the cock, which is 3 feet in length and weighs 51lb.

A *Treatise on Meteorological Instruments*, published in 1860 by Negretti and Zamba, states : " The instrument by which the wind's direction is generally noted, is the vane or weathercock, and all that need be said of it here is that the points, N., E., S. and W., usually attached to it should indicate the true, and not the magnetic directions ; care should be taken to prevent it setting fast." The compass needle points to the magnetic North and not to the true North. The magnetic North varies in the British Isles from approximately 15° West of North in the East of England to about 21° in the West of Ireland. The true cardinal points can be obtained by using a large scale Ordnance Survey map, or the North can be found at night from the Pole Star, and the South by the sun.

Designers of weathervanes should take into consideration when deciding the size of the vane, the height above ground it will be placed, otherwise it may appear too small or too large. In the case of the " dragon " on Bow Church, the correct size was ascertained by first cutting a " relieve in board " which was held in position at the apex of the steeple so that it could be viewed from the ground.

Instructions printed in the *Meteorological Observer's Handbook*, issued by the Air Ministry, state that when erecting a weathervane it must be freely exposed to the wind on all sides and not be affected by local eddies, &c. In using the vane observers should, when ascertaining the wind's direction, stand as nearly as possible under the vane.

23

Weathervanes on Churches

(Introduction)

Church towers and spires, rising above surrounding buildings and trees, provide ideal sites for weathervanes.

It is probable that weathervanes were placed on churches in this land long before they were used on secular buildings.

The most common design in church vanes takes the form of a cock. This bird is associated with St. Peter's denial of Christ (the Gospel according to St. Matthew, Chapter 26, verses 33 to 35, and verses 70 to 75). The cock also symbolises vigilance and watchfulness, necessary attributes of a Christian.

A Papal Bull of the 9th century ordained that a weathercock be placed on every steeple as emblematical of the sovereignty of the church over the whole world, and to remind people of the duty of watchfulness.

Wulfstan, a monk, in the 10th century, saw the re-building of Winchester Cathedral and tells how the mighty tower was crowned by a weathercock. An approximate translation reads : ''. . . to its aspect (of the church tower) is added the golden cock on top of the spire, grand in its adornment and appearance . . . which unceasingly receives from all sides the rain-carrying winds, turning round of its own accord to present to them its face.'' (See Fig. 11, Plate I).

Some churches have vanes in the form of a dragon, the one on St. Mary-le-Bow Church, London, being a well known one, see Fig. 1, Plate IV. In the Revelation of St. John the Divine, Chapter 12, verses 3 to 17, is an account of the great red dragon overthrown by St. Michael and cast out of heaven. In Christian art the dragon has long been used to typify sin.

One of the oldest of Christian symbols, a fish, is also used in church weathervanes, see Fig. 29, Plate VII, and Fig. 38, Plate IX. The initial letters of the Greek words for ''Jesus Christ, Son of God, Saviour,'' form the Greek word for fish. A fish is also a reminder of Christ's parable of the Kingdom of Heaven being like a fishing net. (See St. Matthew's Gospel, Chapter 13, verses 47 and 48).

On churches in coastal towns, vanes in the form of a ship can be seen, as shown in Figs. 46, 49 and 52, Plate X. A few churches have the privilege of surmounting their weathervanes with a crown, see Fig 14, Plate V ; Fig. 18, Plate VI ; and Fig. 28, Plate VII.

The fleur-de-lis (flower of the Lily) is a fairly common form of decoration on church weathervanes. This is used as a symbol of God the Son (called "Lily of the Valley," in Song of Solomon, Chapter II, verse 1).

Many weathervanes on churches are minus the cardinal points. Those responsible for their erection probably assumed that all people are aware of the fact that, lengthways, the chancel and nave face east and west.

Notes on Illustrations
of Weathervanes on Churches

PLATE IV

Fig. 1. The steeple of St. Mary-le-Bow Church, London (considered to be Sir Christopher Wren's most perfect example), has one of the best known weathervanes, a magnificent dragon 8ft. 6in. in length. In records of Wren's churches, 1679, can be read : "To Edward Pearce, mason, for a carving of a wooden dragon for a moddell for ye steeple, and for cutting a relive in board to be profered up to discern the right bigness, the summe of £4.0.0." "To Robert Bird, coppersmith, £38 for making the Dragon." This dragon was probably inspired by the great dragon on the cathedral of St. Bavon, Ghent, Belgium.

Two dragons were adopted as supporters to the City of London Arms about 1633. The dragons may have been introduced in allusion to the legend of St. George.

The following extract is from Sir Walter Besant's *London* : "In sooth-saying we have the prophecy of Mother Shipton that when the Grasshopper on the Exchange (see Fig. 2, Plate XVI), and the Dragon on Bow Church should meet, the streets would be deluged with blood." This improbable meeting actually took place in 1838 when the two vanes were sent to the same yard for repairs, but fortunately the prophecy was not fulfilled. Another prophecy, attributed to J. Swift (b. 1667—d. 1745), refers to the Bow dragon and the weathercock on the Church of St. Bartholomew, by the Exchange (demolished 1841), and reads : "When the Dragon on Bow Church kisses the Cock behind the Exchange great changes will take place in England." According to Hayden's *Table Talk*, just before the passing of the Great Reform Bill of 1832, the Dragon and the Cock were sent to the same works for cleaning and repairs.

PLATE IV

For notes on these vanes see pp. 25 and 27

Fig. 2. Surmounting the tower of Ottery St. Mary Church, Devon, is, should its reputed date, 1335, be correct, the oldest English weathercock, and unlike any other, it "crows." It will be seen that the cock has two trumpet-like tubes running from its breast to its tail, and so arranged that a kind of "crowing noise" is emitted when the wind blows in strength. Since repairs were carried out, the sounds are now more pleasant than those heard previously. This cock may be a copy of the one which was placed on the North Tower of Exeter Cathedral in 1284 (as mentioned in the Fabric Rolls).

Fig. 3. Fordwich, Kent, has this weathervane on its church tower. It bears a resemblance to part of the arms of Sandwich, which consists of "Three demi-lions, passant guardant conjoined to as many demi-hulks of ships in pale." (Fordwich was closely associated with Sandwich in the days of the Cinque Ports). In the Fordwich vane, the part of the ship resembles a 16th century one, and in the accounts of the Mayor of Fordwich in 1588 are these two entries:

"Item—To Brodstrete for takinge downe the vane
      of the steeple and settinge it up againe..   .. 5s. 0d.
Item—To the smythe that mended the vane ..   .. 2s. 0d."

Fig. 4. On a beam in the nave of Alfold Church, Surrey, is preserved this quaintly shaped 16th century cock with one of its tail feathers rusted away. It is doubtful whether another cock like this exists on any other church in the country. A replica of this weathercock has now been placed on the church tower.

Fig. 5. Showing the direction of the wind, on Etchingham Church, Sussex, is the oldest weathervane still in use in this country. Sir William de Echyngham built this lovely 14th century church, and on its tower placed this copper banner-like vane, with ornamental fringe, and pierced with the Echyngham family escutcheon (" a fretty of six pieces "), in A.D. 1387.

Fig. 6. This picturesque vane is on Lambeth Palace, London, and is probably the original one erected A.D. 1663. The pennon has waved points and fleurs-de-lis, and is pierced with the arms of the See of Canterbury, impaled with those of Wm. Juxon, who became Archbishop of Canterbury in 1660. (He attended Charles I to the scaffold when the king was beheaded in 1649).

Fig. 7. This vane displays " The Falcon and Fetterlock," the badge of the House of York. Two of the Dukes of York are buried in the church. It is thought that the vane was placed in position when the beautiful octagonal lantern, which forms the upper part of the tower of Fotheringhay Church, Northamptonshire, was erected in the 15th century. This is obviously one of those vanes whose chief function was to display the badge rather than show clearly the wind's direction.

PLATE V

For notes on these vanes see pp. 29 and 31

PLATE V.

Fig. 8. This 17th century weathervane with pennon shape and having as a pointer a greyhound's head (the crest of Thomas Sutton), is on Charterhouse Chapel, London. The arms, with good Roman letters are supported by elaborate scroll work. Charterhouse was a Carthusian Monastery founded in 1371 by Sir Walter Mannay and Bishop Northburgh, and built over Pardon Churchyard (burial place for persons who died of the plague). In 1611 Thomas Sutton purchased the place to found a hospital for 80 poor and aged gentlemen, a school for 40 poor boys, and a chapel for worship. The school, which later developed into a large public school, moved to Godalming, Surrey, in 1872.

Fig. 9. A griffin is on this 18th century weathervane which surmounts the chapel of Gray's Inn. (A griffin, or gryphon, is a mythical monster, part lion, part eagle, and is supposed to typify strength and vigilance). Gray's Inn is one of the four Inns of Court, London, erected on the site of the old prebendal manor of Portpool, residence of the lords Gray de Wilton, 1315-1505. It passed to the priory of East Sheen, Surrey, who leased it to law students, and it has been the freehold of the Society since 1733. The vane was badly damaged in the air raids of 1941, but a replica will be installed when the building is restored.

Fig. 10. This pennon type of weathervane of the 17th century is pierced with the date and the churchwarden's initials, in good Roman letters, and surmounts the spire of the church at Wadhurst, Sussex. The vane and support, with their decorative scroll work, are very pleasing in design. In the 17th and 18th centuries the district was a famous Sussex iron centre and the church contains 30 fine iron grave-slabs dating from 1614 to 1790.

Fig. 11. This weathercock, its comb, wattle and tail of flat sheet metal, and body shaped by hammering and rivetting two sheets of brass, surmounts the spire of Sheffield Parish Church (now Sheffield Cathedral). The cross on the shaft is uncommon. The tail, which is unusually simple in shape, and the comb of this cock, have scratched upon them a number of names and dates. The Sheffield Church Burgesses, under a Charter granted by Queen Mary, in 1554, are responsible for the repair of the fabric of this church. It has apparently been the custom, when the cock was repaired, for the names of '' The Capitals '' (Chairmen of the Church Burgesses) and builders employed, with dates when the repairs were carried out, to be inscribed on the cock, and the earliest of these dates is 1565. The Church Burgesses' Trust records available do not go back farther than 1565, but there is, however, another date on the tail, i.e., 1428. This may be the year the cock was made, or, should it refer to repairs carried out, then the cock, as its rather primitive shape suggests, is probably a 14th century one.

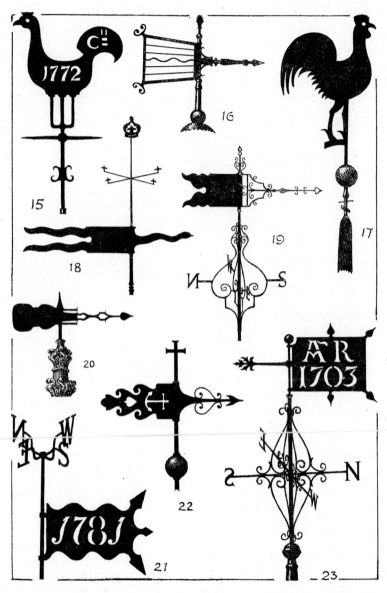

15

16

17

18

19

20

21

22

23

PLATE VI   *For notes on these vanes see pp.* 31, 32 *and* 33

30

Fig. 12. This quaint weathervane with a small cock and curved arm acting as a pointer, is on St. Ethelburga's Church, London. The pierced banner shape contains the date and initials " S.E. ", and has Maltese crosses and fleurs-de-lis. Note the unusual curved arms, on which letters hang. The church escaped the Great Fire, and dates, in its present form, from the 14th or early 15th century. Henry Hudson made his communion in the church before starting on his first voyage in search of the North West Passage.

Fig. 13. This large and very fine 15th century weathercock, unlike the majority, has wings constructed and attached to the body and also has the two legs showing. The tail is finely modelled too. The cock is now on the 15th century tower of Winchcombe Parish Church, Gloucestershire. It was formerly on St. Mary's Church, Redcliffe, Bristol, but was taken down because, apparently, it was too heavy, and brought to Winchcombe about 1880.

Fig. 14. St. Martin's-in-the-Fields Church, Trafalgar Square, London, is one of the few churches having the privilege of placing a crown above its weathervane. St. Martin's is the Royal Parish Church—Buckingham Palace being nearby. The church also had the honour of having King George I as a churchwarden. The church was built 1722-1726, by James Gibbs, and is considered to be his masterpiece. He was a friend and disciple of Sir Christopher Wren. The nicely proportioned vane forms a pleasing finish to the church spire.

PLATE VI.

Fig. 15. This simple conventional shaped cock, appearing to have three legs, with date and letter " C " for Chailey, still faces the winds on the broach spire of the Early English Gothic church in the village of Chailey, Sussex.

Fig. 16. On the Church of St. Lawrence Jewry, in Gresham Street, London, before the building was destroyed during the air raids in 1942, was this unusual weathervane in the form of a gridiron, signifying the death of St. Lawrence who was roasted on a gridiron in A.D. 258.

Fig. 17. In 1818 this alert weathercock replaced the cross on the tall spire on the 13th century tower of Holy Trinity Church, Cuckfield, Sussex. The form of the cock was adapted from the crest of Mr. Clutton, who, at that time, lived in the 17th century house known as " Ockenden." The church has a fine 15th century roof with painted decorations.

Fig. 18. Shows one of the four weathervanes (all similar) on the pinnacles of the ancient Bell Tower at Evesham, Worcestershire. The pointer of the vane is in the form of a swan's neck and head, in fact, the general appearance of the vane is like a conventionalised form of a swan in flight. Tradition states that the four weathervanes were moved from Worcester Cathedral and erected on the Evesham tower 200 years ago, but no confirmation of this exists. May's *History of Evesham* definitely states that the vanes were on the tower in 1760. It will be seen a crown is above the vane. The privilege of using the crown may have been granted by Charles I in gratitude for the townspeople's loyalty. Charles stayed in the town and held court there in 1644. The swan is a Royal bird which may have influenced the designer of the vane. The town was of great strategical importance in the Civil War. Although it changed hands several times it was mostly in Royalist control.

Fig. 19. This is an attractive pennon-shaped weathervane, with delicate and graceful iron scroll design and good Roman letters. The vane has adorned the 15th century tower of Great Barton Church, Suffolk, for very many years.

Fig. 20. This violin-shaped weathervane is on the South East pinnacle of the Perpendicular Gothic Tower of Great Ponton Church, Lincolnshire. The present vane, made locally, is a replica of the original one. There is a legend about the origin of this very unusual church vane ; it relates how a poor fiddler used to play to the villagers, who treated him very kindly. When, later, he managed to get to America and amass a fortune, he remembered the kind villagers and sent them money to build the tower of their church. The weathervane was installed in his memory. This fine tower is, however, stated to have been built in 1519 by one Anthony Ellys, who was Lord of the Manor. (The Manor House is now the Rectory). Ellys was a wool merchant and when he visited Calais he sent home barrels labelled " Calais Sand." In the sand he concealed precious stones of great value, out of the proceeds of the sale of which, the tower was built, so the story goes ; but this does not explain the curious weathervane.

Fig. 21. On the church of St. John-the-Baptist, at Clayton, Sussex, is this 18th century weathervane in the style of very early ones, having no pointer, but fitted with arms and letters indicating cardinal points, placed in the unusual position above the vane. On the walls of the church are very interesting 13th century paintings.

Fig. 22. St. Clement Danes' Church, London, has this weathervane, probably dating from 1719, when the tower was raised to 116 feet. The anchor is a reminder that Saint Clement suffered martyrdom, during the reign of Trajan the Roman Emperor, being thrown into the sea. So that his corpse should not be venerated, it was tied to an anchor and dropped three miles out to sea, but, according to a legend, the sea receded miraculously and so defeated Trajan's object. The other pierced object in the vane, a spade, is accounted for by another legend, which states that while Clement was working in the marble quarries in the Crimea, the prisoners had to walk 6 miles to get water. Then Clement had a vision of a lamb pounding with his foot into the ground. A hole was dug at this spot and water was found.

Fig. 23. At Rye, Sussex, a lovely little town, unlike any other in this country, this beautiful early 18th century weathervane surmounts the ancient tower of St. Mary's Church. The banner-like vane, with fine letters (indicating the reign of Queen Anne), and date, decorative pointer and beautiful iron scroll work forms a most attractive design. The unique possession of the church is a clock, the oldest still in use in England.

PLATE VII

Fig. 24. The church of St. Thomas A'Becket-in-the-Cliff, Lewes, Sussex, has this weathervane embodying the initials of the churchwardens (an old custom of some churches), and the date in a sun-like form on the end of the pennon vane. The church is supposed to occupy the site of a religious house erected to the memory of St. Thomas A'Becket.

Fig. 25. Stanwell Church, Middlesex, has this dated weathervane surmounted by the crest (a head of a white hart) of the family of Lord Windsor. Fitz-Otto, founder of the family and builder of the Manor (see the Domesday Book) was, with his descendants, custodians of Windsor Castle and took the name of Windsor. The title became extinct in the 16th century. The church had a benefaction from Andrew, Lord Windsor, who gave Stanwell to Henry VIII in 1543, in exchange for other lands. The old Manor, much altered, still exists. Note the graceful wrought-iron scroll work on the vane and support.

Fig. 26. This 18th century weathervane on St. Luke's Church, Old Street, London, E.C., has aroused much speculation as to what the design represents. An old theory is that it is a louse, erected by the builder because of some parsimony on the part of the authorities ; thus the church was known as " Lousy St. Luke's." Another view advanced was that the vane represented a comet. (The Great Comet of 1744 was spectacular. There was a brief period when " Comet " vanes were in fashion). The latest theory, probably a correct one, is that the pointer end (which at one time had a red glass eye), represents a dragon's head with forked tongue, and the tail a flaming comet.

Fig. 27. A dated weathervane of most unusual design is on the Church Tower of St. Mary-at-the-Quay, Ipswich. Although the key is not a very attractive design, the delicate iron scroll work below it is most pleasing.

Fig. 28. St. Michael's Church, at Sittingbourne, has a weathervane, erected in 1834, consisting of a fierce-looking dragon, surmounted by a crown, and with a fine iron scroll-work design below. The privilege of using the crown may have reference to the

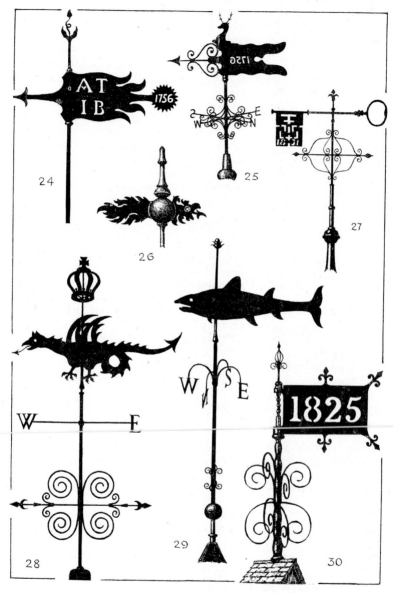

24

1756

25

26

27

28

W————E

29

W S E

30

1825

PLATE VII

For notes on these vanes see pp. 33 and 35

34

fact that Henry V stayed at the ancient Red Lion Inn, as indicated by an advertisement issued by the landlord in c. 1820, and which reads as follows:—"Sittingbourne in Kent, is a considerable thoroughfare on the Dover Road, where there are several good inns particularly the Red Lion, which is remarkable for an entertainment made by Mr. John Norwood, for Henry V as he returned from the battle of Agincourt in France, in the year 1415, the whole amounting to no more than nine shillings and ninepence, wine being at that time only a penny a pint, and all other things being proportionately cheap. P.S. The same character, in a like proportionate degree, Wm. Whitaker hopes to obtain by his moderate charges at the present time."

Fig. 29. This fish weathervane, 5ft. 6in. in length, is on the brick tower of St. John the Baptist Church, Lewes, Sussex. The tower was erected in 1714, and the vane may have been placed on it at the same time. The curved arms, supporting the letters, are unusual, perhaps the designer had seen the vane on St. Ethelburga's Church. (See Fig. 12, Plate V). The church houses leaden coffins containing the remains of William de Warenne and his wife, Gundrada, fifth daughter (?) of William the Conqueror.

Fig. 30. A banner-shaped weathervane, decorated with fleurs-de-lis, date, large iron scrolls under, and having a very nicely shaped terminal on the spindle, is fixed on the small bell-cote of the 17th century brick church at Groombridge, a lovely village on the borders of Kent and Sussex.

PLATE VIII

Fig. 31. While no records of this weathervane, on the church of St. Peter-the-Less, Chichester, Sussex, exist, it appears to have been in position a very long time. The vane is in the form of a wyvern (a representation of a chimerical animal imagined as a winged dragon with two feet like those of an eagle, and serpent-like barbed tail), symbolical of Satan.

Fig. 32. A dove with olive leaf is an uncommon subject for a church weathervane, and this one, nearly 100 years old, is on the tower of St. John-the-Baptist's Church, Crawley, Sussex. Probably the designer had in mind the Bible story of Noah's dove. (See Genesis, Chapter VIII, Verse 11). This vane has a strong local connection, for on occasions, the river overflows its banks and causes flooding in the district.

Fig. 33. A highly decorated weathervane adorns the 14th century tower of St. Mary's Church, Eastbourne, Sussex. The vane, with date and churchwarden's initials, and several fleurs-de-lis, has part of a dragon (symbolic of Satan), for its pointer, reminding people to beware of the tempter's wiles. This vane replaces the one dated 1739, having the churchwardens' initials, E.A. and I.R.,

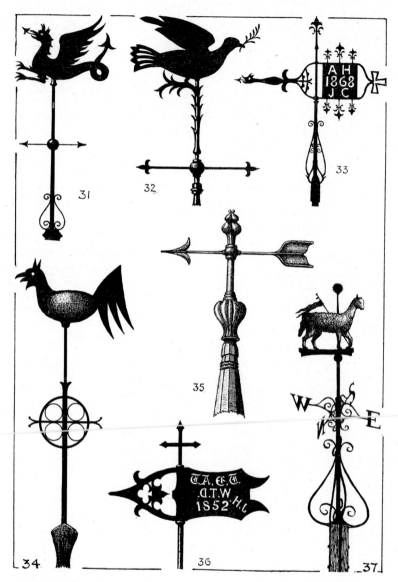

PLATE VIII

For notes on these vanes see pp. 35 and 37

36

and further inscribed " 1790, repaired by C. Gilbert Esq." A part of this old vane is preserved.

Fig. 34. From the top of the 15th century tower of the church at Little Horsted, Sussex, Beachy Head can be seen, and on the roof of the tower is this quaint weathercock with rounded body, unusual tail and Mephistopheles-like head. The iron circles below are pleasing in design.

Fig. 35. Although this is a simple arrow weather vane, it is distinctive because of its decorative embossed copper mounting which is very pleasing in shape. This vane is on the spire of St. Mary's Church, Goring, Sussex. The arms with letters indicating the cardinal points are not included in the drawing as they do not improve the design.

Fig. 36. This is another of the weathervanes pierced with the initials of the churchwardens (T. Arkcott and E. Taylor) and date. The design of the vane, Gothic-like in character, was not improved when the churchwardens from 1908 to 1913 added their initials to be read from the opposite side of the vane which is on All Saints' Church, Herstmonceux, Sussex. The church contains a very fine 15th century tomb, and near the church is the famous brick castle, built in the 15th century and now used by the staff of Greenwich Observatory.

Fig. 37. A vane, built up in a rounded form, showing a lamb with a small flag, on St. Mary's Church, Hendon, London. The use of this design on the church may be due to the following reason : The Knights Templars originally owned much land in this district. When their estates were confiscated, some of the land was acquired by the Knights Hospitallers of St. John of Jerusalem, and their badge embodied a lamb with a flag (Paschal Lamb or " Agnus Dei"). The Knights Hospitallers succeeded the Templars as owners of the Temple, London, and a similar design was used for the vane on the Hall of the Middle Temple, London. In St. John's Gospel, Chapter I, Verses 29 and 36, Jesus is referred to as the " Lamb of God."

PLATE IX

Fig. 38. A very large fish vane, built up in a rounded form, on the spire of the Norman round tower of St. John's Church, Piddinghoe, Sussex. It is referred to in a poem by Rudyard Kipling as follows :—". . . or South, where windy Piddinghoe's begilded dolphin veers." Kipling was indulging in poetic licence, for the fish represents a salmon-trout. The River Ouse, which winds round the base of the hill on which the church stands, was, in bygone days, a salmon river.

Fig. 39. The 19th century church at Eridge, Sussex, has a weathervane with an unusually elaborate pierced design embodying

38 39 40 41 42 43 44 45

PLATE IX   *For notes on these vanes see pp. 37 and 39* a representation of a gate and chains and Tudor rose (part of the arms of the Marquess of Abergavenny) who built the church, and the 19th century castle in the beautiful 1,000-acre Eridge Park.

Fig. 40. Placed on the re-built Wherwell, Hants. Church in 1850, this weathervane, representing a cockatrice (the head, shoulders and legs of a cock, and body, wings and tail of a wyvern), is now in Andover Museum. A local legend regarding the cockatrice dates back to 965, when Queen Elfrida founded a Nunnery at Wherwell. In the cellar of this Nunnery, the story goes, a duck laid an egg which was hatched by a toad, hence the cockatrice. This cockatrice grew to a great size and killed everyone who came near it. However, a woodman named Green, made a large mirror of metal which was lowered on a rope into the cellar, whereupon the cockatrice began to fight its own image. After a week of fierce fighting the monster was so weakened that Green was able to go into the cellar and finish it off. A curious survival of the legend is that in the Harewood Forest there is still a patch of ground called " Green's four acres." A cockatrice is referred to in the Bible (A.V.), see Isaiah, Chapters 11, 14 and 59, Verses 8, 29 and 5, and Jeremiah, Chapter 8, Verse 17.

Fig. 41. On the central tower of the 13th century cruciform church at Ditchling, Sussex, is this gilded weathervane, a simple arrow-like shape with curved ends, but differing from the arrow vane at Goring (See Fig. 35, Plate VIII). Opposite the church is a fine half-timbered house, with outside staircase, which Henry VIII gave to Anne of Cleves.

Fig. 42. The small fishing town of Southwold, Suffolk, has, on the tower of its magnificent medieval church, this weathervane, in the form of a small fishing boat, designed by Mr. Critten (Vicar's Churchwarden), of the Manor House, in 1925. The church, built by rich wool merchants, has three 15th century carved and painted screens, beautiful examples of medieval woodwork.

Fig. 43. This pennon-type vane, with attractive wrought-iron scroll decoration, its age unknown, is on the old tower of Oxted Church, Surrey. The placing of a cock on top of the spindle is unusual, and its naturalistic shape suggests that it was a later addition.

Fig. 44. Surely, no other weathercock has such a gorgeous tail (which overshadows even the fine iron scroll design below), as this one on the modern Church of the Good Shepherd, in Dyke Road, Hove, Sussex.

Fig. 45. This splendid weathervane is on the graceful needle spire of the 20th century Norwegian Church of St. Olav's Kirke, for the use of Norwegian sailors, at Rotherhithe, London. Appropriately enough the vane is a representation of a fine Viking ship supported by beautiful filigree-like iron scroll work.

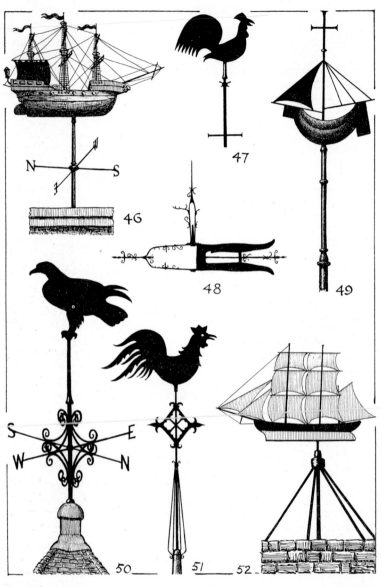

46

47

48

49

50 51 52

PLATE X

For notes on these vanes see p. 41

PLATE X

Fig. 46. " The Missions to Seamen " (Port of London) Institute, erected in 1936, had this splendid weathervane, which was removed for safety during the war. The vane is a fine example of modern craftmanship, and is so constructed that the bows of the ship face the direction the wind is blowing from.

Fig. 47. One hundred and seventy-five feet above the ground, on top of the fine shingled spire, which rests on the 800-year-old tower of St. Mary's Church, Horsham, this vigilant-looking cock turns in the wind. Note the large surface area of the tail to catch the wind.

Fig. 48. This ancient weathervane, made of wrought iron, has now " retired " (rather the worse for wear) from its position on the tower of Rodmell Church, Sussex, and hangs on the wall of the tiny baptistry, which houses a font reputed to be of Saxon origin. An old print of the church shows the vane on the tower in 1850.

Fig. 49. This curious ship, with a cross on its mast, forms the weathervane on the church of Our Lady of Ransom, Eastbourne, Sussex. It was made in 1901 to a design drawn by Mr. Walters, the architect. For a coastal town, a ship is an appropriate subject, and is possibly symbolic of " Peter's ship." There is a certain similarity between this boat and a 14th century " Dromon " as seen in the mosaic design on the ceiling of St. Mark's, Venice.

Fig. 50. When the tower of the fine panelled and richly decorated chapel of St. John's College, Hurstpierpoint, Sussex, was completed in 1930, this weathervane, in the form of an eagle at rest (the eagle being the symbol of St. John), was erected on it. The original design was made from drawings supplied by the London Zoo authorities. This college, with those at Lancing and Ardingly, were founded by Canon Woodard, for the education of the youth in Church of England doctrine and discipline.

Fig. 51. On the low pyramid roof of the 16th century tower of Steyning Church, Sussex, is this handsome weathercock, with an elaborate tail, on a decorative iron support. The church contains some imposing Norman pillars and arches, rich with carving that appears as sharp and clear as in the days it was executed.

Fig. 52. Many ship-type weathervanes are built up in the form of models of the vessel, but this one, on the tower of Nevin Church, Caernavonshire, is cut from sheet metal, painted in two colours, and is so constructed that it moves like a ship running before the wind. In the 19th century sailing ships carried slate from Bangor to the Continent and this seafaring tradition is commemorated by the erection of this vane.

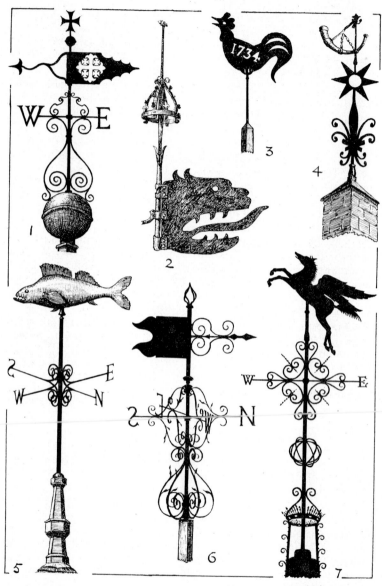

PLATE XI

For notes on these vanes see pp. 43, 44 and 45

Weathervanes on Public Buildings

(*Introduction*)

The above term is used in a wide sense and includes buildings the public can visit, use, or are associated with, such as town halls, schools, museums, sports grounds, &c. Churches are, of course, public buildings, but they are given a section of the book to themselves.

Many public buildings have a cupola, tower, or other part of the roof above the level of the rest of the building which forms a convenient and prominent place for a weathervane.

As in the cases of some business premises, a few public buildings have weathervanes, the designs of which include part or whole of a coat of arms or badge, see Figs. 1 and 7, Plate XI ; Fig. 9, Plate XII and Fig. 19, Plate XIII, while in other vanes the design may suggest the use to which the building is put or its association with the life of the town, &c., see Figs. 10 and 15, Plate XII ; Fig. 20, Plate XIII ; and Fig. 34, Plate XV.

One of the important buildings in every town is the General Post Office. Visitors entering the town often require to use this public office for various purposes and have to enquire as to its whereabouts. The location of churches can be clearly seen by the weathervane on the tower or spire. If the postal authorities would design a distinctive weathervane and erect one on a flagstaff on the General Post Office in each town this would be of much assistance.

Notes on Illustrations
of Weathervanes on Public Buildings

PLATE XI

Fig. 1. Surmounting the octagonal lantern of the 17th century County Hall in the fine old Berkshire town of Abingdon is this attractive weathervane which is contemporary with the building. The vane embodies the arms of the Borough of Abingdon ('' Vert a cross paty gold between four crosses formy silver ''). Note the fine iron scroll design and good Roman letters. The builder of the Hall was Christopher Kempster, of Barford, Oxon., who acted as a master-builder for Sir Christopher Wren in the erection of St Paul's Cathedral, London, and Tom Tower, Oxford.

Fig. 2. Possibly suggested by a vane at Dijon, France, this weird looking head is part of a weathervane preserved in Maidstone Museum, Kent. The pointer and parts of the crown are rusted away. The museum is housed in what was Chillington Manor House, probably built by Nicholas Barham in 1562, on foundations of an older building. It is thought that the vane was on this manor house.

Fig. 3. This dated weathercock is on all that remains of a gibbet (known as " Jacob's Post "), on Ditchling Common, Sussex. Jacob, a Jew, murdered the three inmates of the nearby Royal Oak Inn one night in May, 1734. Jacob was hanged in Horsham Gaol and his body exposed in chains on the gibbet as a warning to other would-be evil doers. Superstitious persons, in by-gone days, believed that they would be magically protected if they touched the gibbet.

Fig. 4. From the 13th century until 1604, the chief officer of Ripon, Yorkshire, was called the " Wakeman." He blew the horn at 9 p.m. each night—a form of curfew. In 1604 the last " Wakeman " became the first Mayor, and an official horn-blower was appointed. This custom of sounding the horn is thought to date back to Alfred the Great. In 1780 Wm. Aislabie, M.P. for Ripon, erected the 90ft. high stone pillar, in the market square, on which is this weathervane, designed to represent the " Wakeman's Horn."

Fig. 5. This vane is on the beautiful little chapel, on the famous 13th and 15th century bridge at Bradford-on-Avon, one of the few remaining chapels once common on English bridges. The chapel was probably used for a priest to say Mass for the soul of the builder ; for in medieval times the building of a bridge was thought to be a very pious deed.

Since the Reformation the chapel has been used for other purposes. At one time it was a " lock-up." An old saying relating to anyone about to be confined in it was :—" He wer agwoing auver the water but under the vish " (i.e., He was going over the water but under the fish). Charles Wesley was one of many prisoners who spent the night locked up in this building. The vane is 16th century work in copper gilt, and the fish represents a " Bradford gudgeon." A fish is one of the very early Christian symbols.

Fig. 6. This 18th century weathervane, now in the Victoria and Albert Museum, London, is a delightful piece of wrought iron scroll work by a highly skilled craftsman, and it is pleasing to know that it is to be preserved in good condition for those who appreciate fine examples of the work of craftsmen of bygone days.

Fig. 7. Destroyed during the 1939-45 war, this splendid weathervane was on the clock tower of the Inner Temple, London. The vane is a beautiful example of the smith's art, with its fine winged horse and delightful wrought-iron scroll design on the support. The Temple was the property of the Knights Templars from 1184 to 1313. This religious order was founded at Jerusalem, c. 1118, members being vowed to chastity, poverty and obedience. '' Pegasus '' (the winged horse) was adopted as the badge of the Knights Templars in the 16th century, and may be a symbolical allusion to the winged horse on which Bellerophon (a type of Christian Knight) fought against the Chimaera (typifying the heathen Turk).

The original seal of the Knights Templars was '' two knights riding a single horse,'' an emblem of poverty. A writer of the early history of the Inner Temple states that the badge of the New Temple, during 120 years in which it was occupied by the Knights Templars, was the seal, but tradition credits an ingenious or ignorant workman, between the 14th and 16th centuries, with altering the horse with the two knights to one with two wings.

In Greek mythology, '' Pegasus '' was the winged horse which sprang from the blood of the Gorgon Medusa when her head was struck off by Perseus. Sir James Thornhill executed a painting in Inner Temple Hall of '' Pegasus Springing from Mount Helican.'' Since 1608 the Temple has belonged to two of the English legal Societies.

PLATE XII

Fig. 8. This very quaint winged beast with a forked tongue and tail indicates the wind's direction day by day on the Town Hall at Maidstone, Kent. The letters showing the cardinal points are of a good type, but the poor and unnecessary decoration on the four arms does not enhance the appearance of the vane.

Fig. 9. Before it sustained the great damage in the 1939-45 war, the fine 15th century London Guildhall had weathervanes as shown by this drawing. The design embodying the City arms and sword has a decorative pointer and pleasing iron work at the base of the support.

Fig. 10. This curious vane is on the British Railways' Fire Station, at Newhaven. The vane at one time adorned the old fire engine, but when the son of a coppersmith, attached to the staff, returned from the Boer War, he was feted by his friends and hauled round the town on the fire engine. Then someone had the idea of detaching the vane from the engine and placing it on the fire station to commemorate the event. The vane has been on the station ever since.

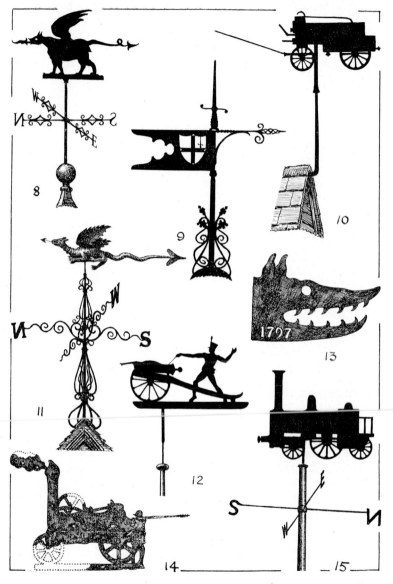

PLATE XII

For notes on these vanes see pp. 45 *and* 47

Fig. 11. A 17th century weathervane, in the form of a dragon, which was originally on the Guildhall (built 1611, pulled down 1828), at Newbury, Berkshire, while the shaft, with graceful scroll decoration and cardinal points, was on the old Cloth Hall (now the museum). When this Hall was restored in 1829 it is thought the dragon was erected on the shaft referred to above. The dragon bears a striking resemblance to the one Sir Christopher Wren put on the steeple of Bow Church, London (see Fig. 1, Plate IV). This raises an interesting point as to whether Wren was responsible for both of the dragons.

Fig. 12. On the Royal United Service Institution flagstaff in Whitehall, London, is this weathervane, of an unusual design, representing a field gun being discharged by a gunner of the Royal Artillery in the uniform of 1800. The vane was formerly on the roof of the Ship Street Barracks in Dublin for more than 120 years. It was given by the Commander-in-Chief in Ireland, in 1922, to the above Institution. Note the spirited and graceful action of the gunner.

Fig. 13. The late Mr. Aymer Vallance, F.S.A., whose book, *Old Crosses and Lychgates*, is so well known, presented this fierce-looking beast's head to the Maidstone Museum, Kent. The head is part of an old weathervane, and the designer of it may have seen the one shown in Fig. 2, Plate XI.

Fig. 14. Bedford Modern School Museum now houses this replica, in sheet iron, of a threshing machine engine. As can be seen by the dotted lines on the drawing, parts are missing, having rusted away. The engine design formed part of a weathervane that a blacksmith at Biggleswade, Bedfordshire, made and erected on his forge about 1840. The drawing was made from sketches by some boys of the school.

Fig. 15. On the town station at Birkenhead, Cheshire, is this 100-year-old weathervane, a silhouette replica in sheet metal of the type of locomotive that brought the first trains to Birkenhead on the Chester and Birkenhead Railway, which was opened in 1840.

PLATE XIII

Fig. 16. Prior to 1912, some telegraph poles, erected in various parts of the country, had weathervanes on top of them, said to have been placed there to placate landlords who were " awkward " over wayleaves. A few of these vanes have survived to the present time, some with parts rusted away, as shown in the drawing of the one on Shedden Hill, Torquay, Devon.

Fig. 17. A very fine model, in copper, of Nelson's ship *Victory*, forms the weathervane mounted on one of the houses named " Nelson " at the Royal Hospital School, Holbrook,

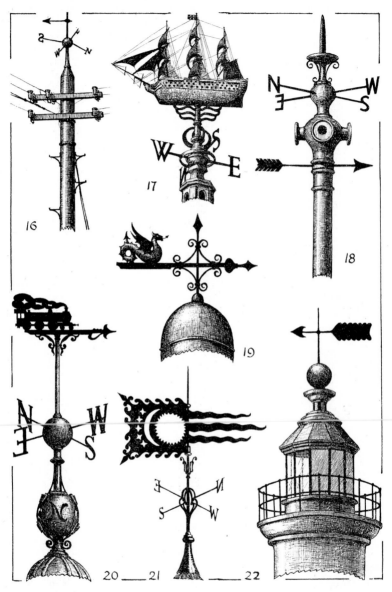

PLATE XIII

For notes on these vanes see pp. 47 and 49

Suffolk. The ship, with support and fine Roman letters is a most attractive object. The Royal Hospital School was, until 1933, at Greenwich, London, S.E. It forms part of the Greenwich Hospital (founded by charter, of King William and Queen Mary, dated October 25th, 1694), when the Royal Palace grounds at Greenwich were converted into a hospital for disabled seamen of the Royal Navy. In 1712 the teaching of sons of seamen commenced with 10 boys. The School at Holbrook was built to accommodate 1,000 boys. The drawing was made by kind permission of the Lords Commissioners of the Admiralty and the architects, Messrs. Bucklands & Haywood, Birmingham.

Fig. 18. There are five iron posts (with weathervanes on them, similar to that shown in the drawing of the top of one of the posts) on the Malvern Hills, Worcestershire. These posts are sewer shafts, or connected with them. A former surveyor of the Council took a great interest in local weather statistics and it is possible that he arranged for the erection of the vanes, although this is merely a surmise. It is certainly a curious position for a weathervane.

Fig. 19. This attractive and nicely designed weathervane embodies a wyvern which has recently been added to the town's coat of arms. The vane is on the cupola of the very fine timber and plaster Guild Hall at Leicester, which was the Hall of the Corpus Christi Guild. The building was used as a Town Hall from 1563 to 1876.

Fig. 20. This large weathervane (overall length of engine and arrow-shaped pointer is 7ft. 6in.) is on the British Railways' North-Eastern Headquarters at York. The original vane, designed by Horace Field, architect for the building, was erected in 1901, but taken down in 1923 and replaced by the present one shown in the drawing. The general design was not altered, but instead of the original tank engine, a silhouette of a B.13 type engine was introduced. The lower part of the support is formed of three beaten copper panels with pierced letters, N.E.R., in them. Fine bold Roman letters are used for the cardinal points.

Fig. 21. The Curator of the Maidstone Museum, Kent, states that this weathervane was made in 1878 for the Observatory tower in the town. The vane has pierced forms representing sun, moon and stars, while the pointer suggests the sun's rays—an appropriate design for such a building.

Fig. 22. Weathervanes on lighthouses are used by the keepers when compiling their weather records. These vanes are constructed to indicate the wind's direction on an interior dial. The vane shown in the drawing is on the land lighthouse, Shoreham Harbour, Sussex. Trinity House, London, who are responsible for the upkeep of lighthouses, do not possess any record of the earliest lighthouse to

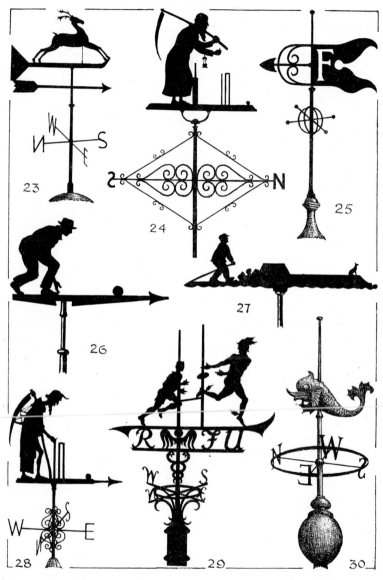

PLATE XIV

For notes on these vanes see pp. 51 *and* 53

be fitted with a weathervane. A vane with a large gilt crown, sur-mounted Eddystone Lighthouse (destroyed in 1703). Engravings, drawn in 1820, show vanes on Douglas Harbour and St. David's Head Lighthouses.

In the Board Room at the Admiralty, Whitehall, London, is an indicator dial worked by a weathervane on the roof. In the days of sailing ships, members of the Board consulted this dial to ascertain whether the wind was favourable before issuing orders for their convoys of ships to sail down Channel.

PLATE XIV

Fig. 23. The College of Matrons, Salisbury, founded by Bishop Seth Ward, provides homes for widows and daughters of clergymen. On the building is this attractive weathervane with a stag and arrow facing the winds. The vane has been in use for more years than the oldest inhabitant can remember. The triangular plate of metal gives a larger surface area for the wind to act upon. The arrow, in addition to pointing to the direction the wind is blow-ing from, is a reminder of the days gone by when it was used by archers hunting the animals for food.

Fig. 24. This wrought-iron weathervane, made by a prisoner, in 1935, is on H.M. Prison, Lewes, Sussex, and replaces the former arrow-shaped vane. It is evident that the prisoner was a skilled metal-worker and that he was acquainted with the " Father Time " vane at Lord's Cricket Ground, London (see Fig. 28). Although choosing the same subject, the prisoner did not slavishly copy the Lord's vane. His figure, inferior to the Lord's one, symbolises the man in prison " doing time," while the removed bail signifies that, once sentenced and sent to prison, there is " no bail " for him. Below the vane are the words : " Time will bail you out." The attractive scroll design is too large in proportion to the figure above.

Fig. 25. The design of this pennon-type of weathervane is pleasing, with graceful lines and proportions, and was erected in 1892 on the fine Village Hall at Forest Row, Sussex. The hall was built by Mr. H. R. Freshfield, of Kidbrooke Park, in memory of his son.

Fig. 26. This weathervane, depicting a bowls player in action, can be seen at Preston Park, Brighton, where bowlers congregate all through the summer. As a strong wind has an effect on the "woods" being rolled up, the weathervane serves a useful purpose.

Fig. 27. The design of this weathervane is uncommon, representing a river barge with " bargee " and his dog on board. The vane is on the tower of the splendid Guildhall at Kingston-upon-Thames, Surrey. The architect used this design as symbolic of the town's close association with the River Thames.

PLATE XV

For notes on these vanes see pp. 53 and 54

52

Fig. 28. The "Father Time" weathervane, erected above the scoreboard at Lords, the famous home of the Marylebone Cricket Club, was designed by Sir Herbert Baker, the architect, and presented to the Club in 1925. "Father Time," represented by a lean, gaunt old figure, with his scythe and hour-glass, in the act of removing the bails, signifies the end of a team's innings or close of the day's play, and also reminds each of us that our life's innings on earth must come to an end when our "time" is up.

Fig. 29. On one of the buildings at the Rugby Football Union's ground at Twickenham, Middlesex, is this large weathervane, 8ft. 3in. in length, designed by Mr. K. Daiglish, F.R.I.B.A., and made by Messrs. Comyn Ching & Co., London. The design shows the figure of Hermes, the swift-footed messenger of the Greek gods, passing the ball to a young footballer near the goal posts. Under these figures is a wand with wings and twined serpents. A golden wand was presented to Hermes by Apollo who stated that it possessed the faculty of uniting in love all beings divided by hate. Wishing to prove the truth of this assertion, Hermes threw it down between two snakes which were fighting, whereupon the angry combatants clasped each other in loving embrace, and curling round the wand, remained ever after permanently attached to it. The wand typified power ; the serpents, wisdom ; and the wings, despatch. A vane on a football ground serves a most useful purpose by showing the captain of the team winning the "toss," the direction the wind is blowing from, so that he can decide whether to play with or against it at the start of the game.

Fig. 30. On the south bank of the River Thames is the fine County Hall of London, designed by Ralph Knott (an old boy of the City of London School and a pupil of Sir Aston Webb), who won the competition for which hundreds of architects entered. The foundation stone was laid by King George V on March 9th, 1912. The weathervane on this hall consists of a picturesque dolphin, having more graceful lines and proportions than the one shown in Fig. 31, Plate XV. Note the unusual mounting of the fine Roman-type letters which indicate the cardinal points. As dolphins are found round the English coast and occasionally in the River Thames, this fact may have influenced the designer of the vane.

PLATE XV
Fig. 31. Dolphins form part of the Brighton, Sussex, coat of arms, and one, built up in a rounded form, is used on this weathervane on the Brighton and Hove Grammar School. The vane and its support are made of copper and exposure to the sea air has turned the surface of the copper a lovely pastel shade of green which, against the blue sky, has a most pleasing appearance. The decorative style used for the letters makes them less easy to read than Roman or block letters.

Fig. 32. Above the Town Hall of Watlington, Oxfordshire (built 1664), is this weathervane with a rather crude design of a dragon's head. No information is available as to when the original vane was erected, but the date was probably much earlier than an 1823 print showing it on the Town Hall. Dragon vanes can be found on several very old buildings. The present vane is an accurate replica of the original one, and was made by a local blacksmith, Mr. Trindall, in 1908. When, in that year, the Town Hall was repaired, the old vane was found to be in too bad a condition for restoration.

Fig. 33. This large and very fine copper model of the *Santa Maria*, the caravel in which Columbus sailed to America in the 15th century, forms the weathervane on the Incorporated Accountants' Hall (formerly Lord Astor's Estate Office), Victoria Embankment, London. The sails are represented as being furled, except the one at the stern, which is fixed in position so that the wind will turn the vessel for the bowsprit to face the direction the wind is blowing from. The scroll design on the support is attractive.

Fig. 34. The Town Hall of Andover, Hants, was re-built in 1825, and this weathervane was erected over it. The lion and oak tree forms part of the town's unofficial coat of arms, and has been used on official documents in the form of a seal since A.D. 1300. In medieval times this area was a forest and the favourite hunting place of kings.

Fig. 35. Totnes, Devon, was a walled town in medieval times, and the North and East gateways still remain. Over the East gateway is a fine panelled room with a coloured frieze and on the chimney-piece are two heads, thought to be of Henry VIII and one of his wives. Surmounting the roof over this room is this pennon-type weathervane somewhat dwarfed by the elaborately decorated support.

Fig. 36. This lovely four-masted sailing ship is a weathervane that must delight the poor maimed and crippled children who spend years of their life at the Heritage Craft Schools at Chailey, Sussex. The vane, a gift of Sir Michael Hodges, is a beautifully constructed model of the *Great Harry* (King Henry VIII's warship of 1,000 tons, which cost £14,000 and was the first double-decked warship constructed in England). The vane was erected under the direction of the architect, Sir Sebastian Comper, above the school's hall on the completion of the building in 1932. How proud Mrs. Kimmins must be of her life's work at Chailey for these crippled children.

Fig. 37. The London County Council open-air school at Charlton, in South-East London, has, on a tall flagstaff, this weathervane, designed and made by Mr. F. J. Martin, a teacher of handicrafts. The vane depicts one feature of the school's activities, the pointer having at its end a form representing the rising sun, which has a lead weight attached to it to balance the vane.

Weathervanes on Business Premises

(*Introduction*)

Some weathervanes on business premises, in addition to showing the direction of the wind, are designed to act as a trade sign, either as a direct pictorial indication of the nature of the business carried on in the building, see Figs. 4, 14, 16, 29, 33, 34, 36, 49, 51, 53 and 55, on Plates XVI to XXIV ; or the vane embodies the whole or part of a coat of arms, thus forming a distinguishing sign for the offices of the company, see Figs. 9 and 12, Plate XVII, and Figs. 41 and 44, Plate XXII. These double-purpose vanes can also be seen on some public buildings and private dwellings.

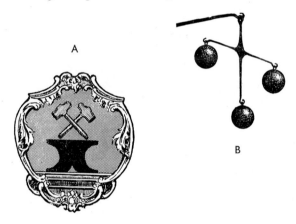

The use of trade signs goes back to ancient times. During the excavations of the ruined cities of Pompeii and Herculaneum, tradesmen's signs have been revealed, such as carved or painted ones representing a '' goat '' on a dairy—carpenter's '' chisel and adze '' —'' ears of corn and millstone '' on a baker's premises, &c. For hundreds of years, owing to the illiteracy of the majority of the people, trade signs were necessary, and continued in this country until mid-eighteenth century times. Some of the common signs in use included the '' coloured pole and basin '' of the barber surgeon —the cutler's '' knife ''—the tailor's '' shears ''—'' lock and hinge '' at the ironmongers—'' hammer and hand '' of the gold beaters—'' three golden balls '' hanging outside the pawnbrokers' premises, &c. The illustrations (A and B) show two of these old

55

signs used by pawnbrokers and anvil-makers. Few of these old signs exist to-day, but occasionally some modern signs can be seen such as the very fine one (C), which is outside the ironmonger's and black-smith's premises at Heathfield, Sussex. These trade signs of past ages may have suggested the use of the double-purpose weathervanes referred to previously.

c

The design of some weathervanes portray the name of the build-ing they are erected on, see Fig. 43, Plate XXII and Figs. 48 and 52, Plate XXIII.

Before the days of the B.B.C. weather reports, farmers learned to forecast weather conditions in their own area by observing the conditions of sky, barometric pressure, wind, &c., so that weather-vanes were most useful to them. Even in these days when the B.B.C. forecasts cover a wide area, local conditions vary, and thus farmers would still find their vanes helpful.

By using a vane representing a cow, chickens or other subject, the farmer could indicate whether his business was a dairy farm, &c., see Fig. 32, Plate XX ; Figs. 54 and 60, Plate XXIV and Fig. 62, Plate XXV.

Notes on Illustrations
of Weathervanes on Business Premises

PLATE XVI

Fig. 1. It is very probable that no other weathervane like this can be seen in this country. The vane is carved from a piece of oak (sleigh, men and pointer stained brown), and represents a sleigh and two men drawn by a team of dogs. It is on a 16th century house at Warren Farm, Chailey, Sussex, and has been in its present position for more than 120 years. Did the son of a former farmer take part in some Arctic expedition ?

Fig. 2. On the Royal Exchange in the City of London is this very famous 16th century weathervane in the form of a grasshopper the badge of Sir Thomas Gresham, who founded and built the Royal Exchange, 1564-1570. Twice, in 1666 and 1838, the building was destroyed by fire and subsequently re-built, the present one in 1844 ; but the grasshopper vane, which is 11 feet long, survived both disasters to crown the third building which was opened by Queen Victoria. The original building was opened by Queen Elizabeth. There is a legend which states that Sir Thomas Gresham was a foundling who was discovered by a woman in consequence of the chirping of a grasshopper, and brought up by her. The badge is also used by Martin's Bank, said to have been founded by Sir Thomas Gresham. Note.—The ancients used the grasshopper as a fascinum (fascination, enchantment) worn about the person to bring good luck.

Fig. 3. The monumental mason, Mr. C. F. Bridgman, although his knowledge of his building in Lewes, Sussex, goes back very many years, does not know the age of this weathervane (a pheasant on a support with decorative scroll work and good Roman style letters). It is not known also why a pheasant was chosen for the vane on such a business building.

Fig. 4. A blacksmith in Uckfield, Sussex, made this weathervane as a sign for his forge, over 100 years ago. It now swings in the wind on a flagstaff in front of a garage at Five Ash Down, Sussex. The owner purchased the vane as a memento of his friendship with the old blacksmith.

Fig. 5. This truly magnificent weathervane (a dragon in flight, on a support surrounded by a beautiful filigree-like wrought-iron scroll work with fine Roman-style letters ; a piece of work that any metal craftsman might be proud of surmounts the dome of the Central Market, Smithfield, London, built in 1868, on the site of the old jousting field. Nearby, martyrs were burned at the stake because they were true to their faith, and London's Lord Mayor slew the rebel, Wat Tyler, in 1381. About 1633 dragons were adopted as supporters of the City arms.

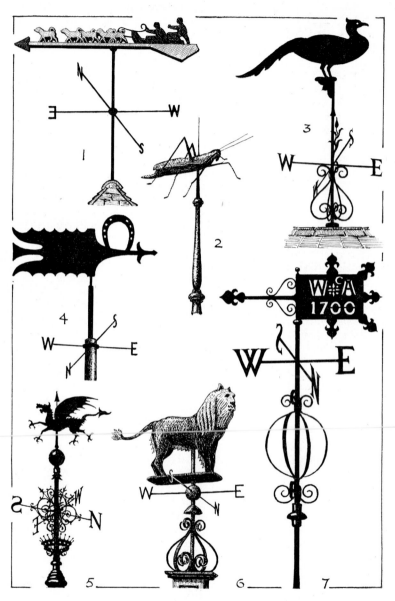

PLATE XVI

For notes on these vanes see pp. 57 *and* 59

Fig. 6. A large weathervane, with the lion built in solid form, is on the Black Lion Brewery, Brighton, Sussex (the oldest one in the town). The building is also probably the oldest in Brighton. The vane is said to have been erected by a Flemish refugee, Deryk Carver, in the 16th century. The wall under the vane bears the tablet to Carver's memory. He introduced a new method of brewing into this country in 1545. He was burned at the stake in front of a house, "The Signne of the Starre," Lewes, July 22nd, 1555, because of his religious beliefs. The vane represents the "Black Lion of Flanders," and a condition of the lease of the brewery is that tenants have to keep the vane in good repair.

Fig. 7. The museum at Walthamstow, Essex, now houses this decorative flag-like weathervane. The vane was originally on a barn at Wadham Farm, which was part of the Wadham Lodge Estate, left to Wadham College, Oxford, in 1652, by John Goodridge, a fellow of that College. The museum authorities have not been able to trace the owner of the initials, W.A., pierced in the vane. The letter C, which spoils the design, is evidently a later insertion. This illustration is from a drawing of the vane made for a lantern slide by Miss A. R. Hatley, the assistant curator at the museum.

PLATE XVII

Fig. 8. Constructed in a partly rounded form, this very fine bronze weathercock faces the winds from its position above the old barn at Gallops Farm, Westmeston, Plumpton, Sussex. The cock is much more naturalistic in appearance than the majority of weathercocks, and is at least 50 years old. It has a few holes in it, due to some person not appreciating its beauty and using it for gun practice.

Fig. 9. On the stables of a 17th century house, "Ockenden," Cuckfield, Sussex, is the crest of the Burrell family serving as a weathervane. The crest is described as "an arm, embowed, ppr, holding a branch of laurel, vert." Note the unusual form of the supports for the cardinal letters. The house was the home of Timothy Burrell in the 17th century. One of his ancestors was vicar of Cuckfield Church. The house is now used as a hotel.

Fig. 10. The present owners of Belmoredean Farm, West Grinstead, Sussex, do not know how long this weathervane has been in position on one of the farm buildings, nor do they know what the queer bird is supposed to be, but it bears some resemblance to a pheasant.

Fig. 11. This is a strange form of weathervane to find on the barn at Swain's Farm, Littleworth, near Partridge Green, Sussex. The present owners of the lovely old farmhouse found the vane in position when they took over the farm. Perhaps a former owner was interested in railways. The old type of locomotive suggests that the vane was made many years ago.

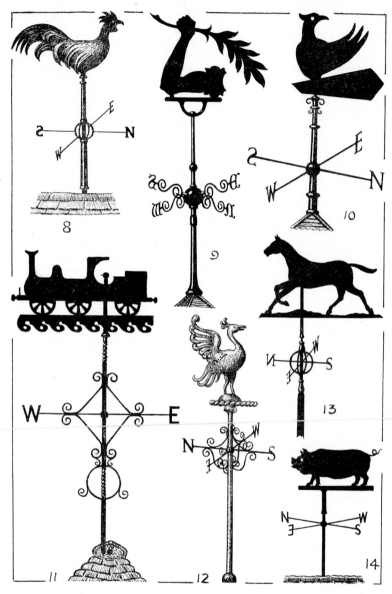

PLATE XVII

For notes on these vanes see pp. 59 *and* 61

Fig. 12. The curious-looking bird forming the vane on the office of the Royal Insurance Company at Brighton, Sussex, is the " Liver " bird. The bird is a myth, and owes its origin to the poor skill of the engravers of the original Corporate Seal of Liverpool. It is intended to represent an eagle—the eagle of St. John the Evangelist—adopted as a compliment to King John, who created Liverpool a Borough in 1207. The above Company was formed in Liverpool in 1845.

The weathervane has been on the Brighton office for 45 years. The bird is of copper, built up in a rounded form, and has very graceful lines. The letters are good Roman ones with pleasing scroll supports.

Fig. 13. A man who has ridden horses since his 7th birthday and recently lost his fine old roan horse after it had given him pleasure for 29 years, erected this " trotting horse " weathervane on a pole in his field on the Brighton Road, Worthing, Sussex. He has another vane, a fox, in front of his house. He, his father, and grandfather, all had a fondness for erecting weathervanes on their premises.

Fig. 14. A pig is an uncommon form of weathervane. This one used to be on a bacon factory at Elmham, Norfolk, and thus acted as a trade sign as well. The factory is now owned by Messrs. Seaman & Sons, millers and merchants, but they do not know what became of the vane.

PLATE XVIII

Fig. 15. Mr. Wise, owner of the Robin Hood Garage, near Patcham, Sussex, made this quaint weathervane 25 years ago. The vane shows the policeman looking at his watch and raising his hand to stop the motorist. The garage is on a part of the London to Brighton road, where, some years ago, the police set traps to catch " speed merchants " who exceeded the limit. Many motorists found themselves having to pay fines.

Fig. 16. This vane, in the form of a dolphin, is on Billingsgate Market, and acts as an appropriate trade sign. The scroll work, with leaf forms, is a graceful design. The Market, situated on the North bank of the River Thames, below London Bridge, is the oldest in London, and probably dates from the 9th century. All kinds of fish are sold there.

Fig. 17. At Hurstpierpoint, Sussex, is a fine old farmhouse. In the grounds is " Stable Cottage," a cosy bungalow, constructed from the stables of the farm, on the top of which is a small lantern-like structure, and surmounting this is a splendid game cock, in an aggressive attitude, turning his face to every wind. The craftsman who made it has done a fine job and produced a cock bristling with life and alertness. The vane was on the farm building long before its conversion into a private dwelling.

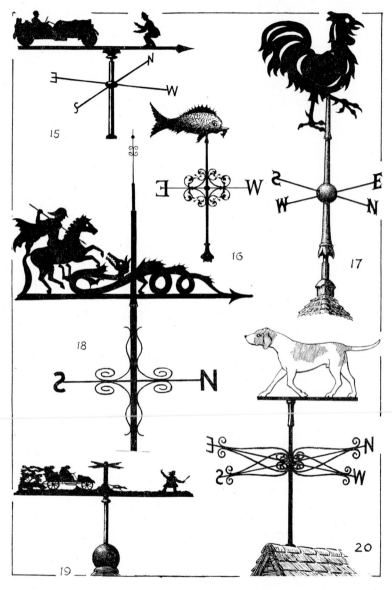

PLATE XVIII

Fig. 18. St. George and the dragon is an uncommon subject for a weathervane, and such a lengthy dragon too ; note how its tail forms the pointer of the vane. This vane is on the cupola of a building in the High Street, Tonbridge, Kent, now occupied for business purposes by Timothy Whites & Taylors Ltd., and was in position when they took over the shop.

Fig. 19. This quaint vane, depicting a sign post, with a policeman holding up the old car (to save the dog's life ?), has been for 30 years on the tower of the garage of Swain & Jones Ltd., Farnham, Surrey. This building was used in bygone days for building coaches and carts which were erected on the upper floors and let down into the forecourt by means of an outside crane. In those days the tower was surmounted by a sign (coach and horses). Note the variation of treatment of Figs. 15 and 19.

Fig. 20. Originally on the residence of the Earl of Chichester, Stanmer Park, Sussex, this foxhound weathervane was purchased by a farmer and erected on his cart shed at Overs Farm, Barcombe, Sussex, but the hound appears much too large in its present position. In its original place on the house at Stanmer Park it was in a much higher position and would look the correct size there. The hound is painted white with brown markings. The shape of the supports for the letters is uncommon.

PLATE XIX

Figs. 21, 22, 26, 27 and 28. These objects, while they cannot be strictly termed weathervanes, are all constructed to use the wind to operate them. Fig. 21 shows the top part of a windmill called the "cap," with the "sweeps" or "sails," while the fan-tail is shown on the right. The working of this fantail is as follows : It is mounted on the " cap," at right-angles to the " sweeps " and the wind causes it to revolve and thus turn the " cap " (which is mounted on a circular rail), until the " sweeps " are square with the wind, which will then cause the " sweeps " to turn and thus operate the machinery to grind the corn.

Fig. 26 shows the top part of the conical roof of an oast house at Beltring, Kent, the county famous for its hop growing gardens. Fitted to the roof is the moveable cowl, and attached to this is a vane, so that the wind can turn the cowl round to the best position to allow the fumes of the fuel, used to dry the hops, to escape freely. The small ornamental feature is quite a common one. Fig. 27 is the vane on the oast house near Hawkhurst, Kent, with a bird used as a decoration ; while the design used on the vane (Fig. 28) on the oast house at Bounds End Farm, Staplehurst, Kent, is a shire horse made by the Staplehurst blacksmith, Mr. Nicholson (Harris & Son),

PLATE XIX

For notes on these vanes see pp. 63 *and* 65

from a drawing by Mr. F. J. Martin. Another piece of decoration on the vane on an oast house is seen in Fig. 22. This very quaint form (a maltster with his shovel) is on the vane attached to the cowl of the old malt house at Aldbourne, Wiltshire. The village was the subject of a B.B.C. broadcast. A local historian of the village states that there is no reference to this curious vane prior to 1838. These decorative features also provide a larger surface area for the wind to act upon.

Fig. 23. On the garage of a farm, this appropriately designed weathervane can be seen near North Chailey Common, Sussex. The horses and man leading them are full of action and skilfully portrayed.

Fig. 24. Another farm weathervane, showing an 18th century farmer seeking the wild fowl to stock his larder. The vane was made by Messrs. Rowland Ward, of London, for the stables of Hankham Hall, Pevensey, Sussex. (Pevensey Marshes are in the district).

Fig. 25. Blacksmiths, in this age of " mechanised farms " have to be prepared to help the farmers when tractors break down ; the smith on the road near Henfield, Sussex, advertises, by his weathervane of a tractor and plough which he made, that he is able to give assistance to those in trouble.

PLATE XX

Fig. 29. Depicting a mare and foal in action, this weathervane on Court Lodge Stud Farm, near Plumpton, Sussex, acts as an advertisement. The graceful lines of the animals are pleasing.

Fig. 30. This farm weathervane is on the oasthouse of " Coopers Green House,", Uckfield, Sussex. The grouping of the horses and man is most attractive. The vane was designed by Miss Thomas, of Buxted, and made by the Lion Green Works Ltd.

Fig. 31. The design of this weathervane, which is on Crab Farm, Shapwick, Dorset, is unique. As far as can be ascertained the vane was made about 1865, and was the outcome of a local legend, which reads as follows :—Many years ago, on the Downs at Badbury Rings, a shepherd did spy a great crab, probably dropped by a fisherman who had passed that way. Not having seen a crab before, the shepherd dashed off to the village to spread the news about the great monster he had seen. The alarmed villagers, armed with pitchforks, sticks, &c., and the oldest inhabitant taken in a wheelbarrow, marched to the Downs. The sight of the large crab amazed them and so frightened the oldest inhabitant that he shouted, " Wheel me off, wheel me round, wheel me back to Shapwick town,

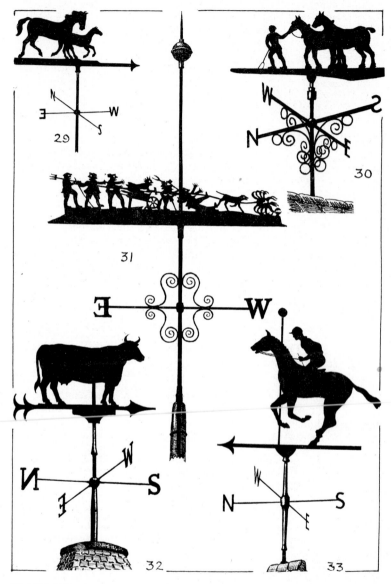

PLATE XX

For notes on these vanes see pp. 65 and 67

or we be all dead men." All dashed back to the village and locked themselves in. The design and workmanship of the vane is a particularly fine piece of imaginative work. Notice the expressions of alarm of the faces of the villagers, the one nearest the crab falling down with fright, while the little hair possessed by the oldest inhabitant, stands on end. The dog is the bravest one in the group. The legend was used by the B.B.C. in their broadcast talk about the village in the " County Mixture " programme dealing with Dorset.

Fig. 32. Stairs Farm, Hartfield, Sussex, where the previous owner kept a pedigree herd of Friesian cows, has this weathervane, a Friesian cow on an arrow, which is a good piece of work by a blacksmith, and has been in position since 1929.

Fig. 33. The breeding of race horses is carried on at High Hurst Stud Farm, Cowfold, Sussex, and, on one of the buildings is this attractive and appropriate weathervane. The motive of the design was copied from a photograph of one of the horses named " Appleby " (ridden by the famous jockey, Steve Donoghue), which won the Bedford Stakes, at Newmarket, in May, 1923.

PLATE XXI

Fig. 34. Another appropriate " trade-sign " weathervane on what used to be the blacksmith's shop of Mr. J. Penrose, in Place Lane, Seaford, Sussex. The internal combustion engine is displacing the horse and so closing down some blacksmiths' shops in towns.

Fig. 35. This weathervane, made in 1898, on the premises of Messrs. Duke & Ockenden, Littlehampton, Sussex, takes the form of a wheel with vanes, which, turned by the wind, is used on pumps to draw water from wells in parts of the country where mains water is not available. As the wind's power is free, the cost of operating the pump, once installed, is negligible. The firm makes these pumps.

Fig. 36. A business-sign weathervane that turns over a house which was the residence of a veterinary surgeon at Lindfield, Sussex, takes the form of a spaniel dog. The scroll work is attractive, and the cardinal points are indicated by finely-proportioned Roman-style letters.

Fig. 37. The son of Mr. Nye, a builder and decorator, made this attractive weathervane, a naturalistic-looking pheasant, for the owner of Birches Farm, Isfield, Sussex. Note the bird's claws gripping the top of the ball and fine Roman-style letters.

Fig. 38. The wife of Mr. Huxtable, the owner of Toat Fruit Farm, near Pulborough, Sussex, designed this weathervane for her husband who is fond of wild fowl shooting, which can be indulged in on the marshes at Pulborough. The vane was made by Spooner & Gordon, of Horsham. The flying birds are graceful in form.

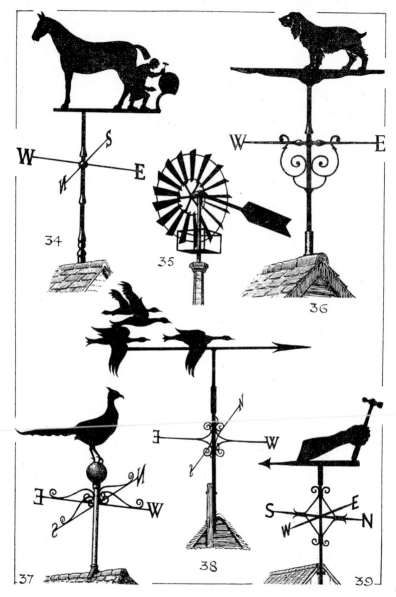

34

35

36

37

38

39

PLATE XXI

For notes on these vanes see pp. 67 *and* 69

Fig. 39. Mr. Mitchell, of Faygate, Sussex, who still turns out very fine decorative wrought-iron work, made this unusual weather-vane and mounted it on his workshop. He says the design illustrates the old Sussex saying :—'' By hammer and hand, all things do stand.'' A blacksmith with his hammer can certainly do good work that lasts for many years as many old weathervanes show.

PLATE XXII

Fig. 40. This huntsman weathervane is mounted on a post outside The Galley Pot Inn at Galleypot Street, Sussex. In the bar of the inn hangs the red coat, top hat, whip and horn that was once the property of the first whip of the Surrey and Burstow Hunt. This inn is the oldest " free house " in England, kept solely in one family for 400 years. Earthenware galley pots, made by hand, with the pattern stamped on them, from $\frac{1}{2}$-pint sizes upwards used to be made in the village.

Fig. 41. A beaver, part of the coat-of-arms of the Hudson's Bay Company, forms the design of the weathervane erected in 1927 on the Company's buildings, 52-68 Bishopsgate, London. The beaver and arrow weigh 80lb., yet the vane is so delicately balanced that a man can blow it round. The scroll design is beautiful, with letters of good shape. The premises were sold to another firm in 1948.

Fig. 42. Lewes, Sussex, has an important race course, and this vane is on a building which was once part of the training stables for race horses, but has now been converted into Mansfield's Astley Garages. The vane has recently been painted in naturalistic colours. It is made of sheet metal.

Fig. 43. Over Messrs. Edlins Ltd., " King and Queen " Hotel, Marlborough Place, Brighton, Sussex, is this striking weather-vane with figures representing King Henry VIII and one of his wives. The vane points to the direction the wind is blowing from and also acts as a sign. The hotel was once a farmhouse, but was called the " King and Queen " in 1779, and was one of the oldest public houses in Brighton. It was pulled down and re-built about 1930.

Fig. 44. This distinctive weathervane has been over the premises of the Leathersellers' Company, at 9 St. Helen's Place, London, E.C.3, since 1930. On the arrow is the head of a demi-roebuck, the crest of the Company's coat-of-arms. The beautiful wrought-iron scroll design and fine Roman-style letters add much to this very attractive design.

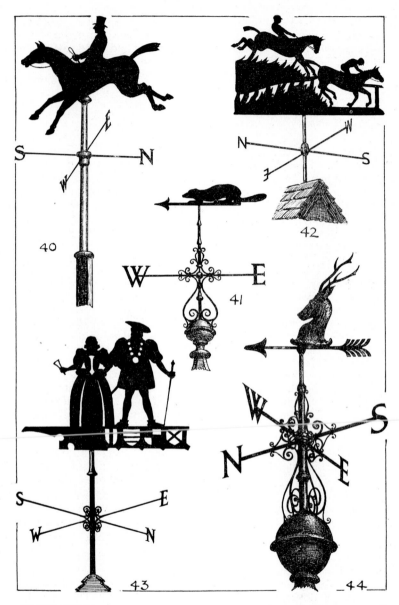

PLATE XXII

For notes on these vanes see p. 69

70

PLATE XXIII

Fig. 45. A weathervane depicting a horse scampering round a field is one to give pleasure to a farmer who is a lover of these animals. This vane is on a barn at Old Park Farm, near Maplehurst, Sussex.

Fig. 46. During the war of 1939-1945, the old blacksmith at Partridge Green, Sussex, saw hundreds of aeroplanes pass over his forge, and amused himself in his leisure hours by making this weathervane for his workshop roof.

Fig. 47. Farmers seem to be very fond of weathervanes in the form of a fox. Perhaps they want a constant reminder to make their poultry secure against their enemy. This fox is on the barn at Roger's Farm, Wivelsfield, Sussex, and appears to be in a hurry to escape its hunters. While fox vanes are common, it is rare to find two similar in design.

Fig. 48. This weathervane, depicting a pheasant, with some fine wrought-iron scroll work, is on the " Pheasant Hotel," Winterslow, Wiltshire, which has been much altered from those days when it was an old coaching inn. William Hazlitt (1778-1830), the well-known British essayist and critic, often stayed at the inn, and wrote his *Winterslow Essays* here.

Fig. 49. Made to represent a terrier, a winner of championships, this weathervane at Littlebury, near Storrington, Sussex, calls attention to the kennels where the terriers are bred. The mounting of the letters of the cardinal points is uncommon and is similar to the one shown in Fig. 49 on Plate XXXII.

Fig. 50. This simple, but graceful, ship with a nice shaped pointer adorns the gable of the shop of a dealer in antiques, at 12 Springfield Road, Horsham, Sussex.

Fig. 51. This is another weathervane calling attention to the species of dogs (Dalmatian) bred at the kennels at North Hall, Staplefield, Sussex. The vane was made by Mr. Boniface, the local blacksmith. This is a case where the painting of the vane makes the breed of the dog more easily recognisable.

Fig. 52. Turning in the wind, for more than 100 years, above the lovely 15th century " Dog and Partridge " Inn at Bury St. Edmonds, Suffolk, is this quaint weathervane (a dog arrested by the sight of a partridge in the grass). Minus cardinal points, the vane was probably erected primarily as a sign to indicate the name of the Inn.

Fig. 53. This " trade-sign " weathervane turns with the wind over the garage at Henfield, Sussex. The style of the saloon car gives its approximate date. Note the neat mounting of the letters.

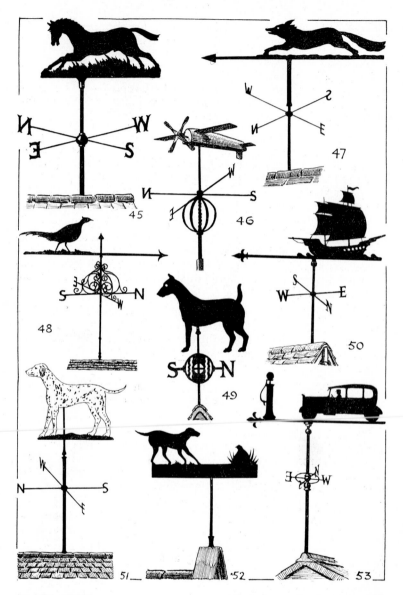

PLATE XXIII

For notes on these vanes see p. 71

PLATE XXIV

Figs. 54 and 57.   Messrs. Bish & Green, sheet metal workers of Shoreham-by-Sea, Sussex, made the weathervane showing a galleon, with a dolphin swimming in front acting as the pointer of the vane (see Fig. 57), for an attractive '' trade-sign '' vane on their workshop. This firm also made the weathervane shown in Fig. 54 for a farmer client from a design supplied by the Rural Industries Bureau.

Fig. 55.   For many years now gas companies have used the quaint figure of '' Mr. Therm '' as their symbol.   The architect of the showrooms at Haywards Heath, Sussex, made use of the figure for the weathervane over the building.   The cardinal points are indicated by good Roman letters supported by a scroll design.

Fig. 56.   The '' baying '' foxhounds form the weathervane on the building at High View Farm, Sussex.   The vane is minus the cardinal points.

Fig. 58.   The pointer end of this weathervane on one of the buildings at Rowden Farm, Frant, Sussex, is weighted to balance the hay waggon, horse and farm labourer, at the other end.   The design would have been more pleasing and balanced in appearance if the man and part of the horse were on the right of the spindle of the vane.

Fig. 59.   This most unusual type of weathervane, made of wood and painted green and white, was made by the Staplefield blacksmith, Mr. Boniface, and erected in the garden of his house at Handcross, Sussex.   The cardinal points are indicated on the circular disc below the figure and direction of the wind shown by a metal rod under the arrow end of the vane.   The figure's arms are made to turn by the action of the wind.

Fig. 60.   This '' Jersey cow '' weathervane is on the barn at Brook Farm, near Cowfold, Sussex, and is painted to show clearly the breed of cows kept at the farm.

Fig. 61.   The Worshipful Company of Farriers, dating from 1356, as a fraternity, was granted its first charter in 1685.   Mr. Carley, the blacksmith at Adversane, Sussex, is a proud member of the Company.   When King George VI was crowned on May 12th, 1937, Mr. Carley designed and made this weathervane and erected it on his forge.   The scroll design is pleasing.

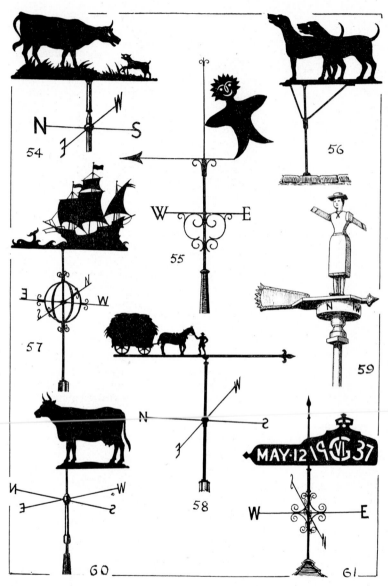

PLATE XXIV

For notes on these vanes see p. 73

PLATE XXV

Fig. 62. As it plainly indicates, this weathervane is erected on a farm building where the rearing of chickens is an important part of the work at Coneyhall Farm, near Pilt Down, Sussex. It was on Pilt Down in 1911 that Mr. Dawson, a Lewes solicitor, came across a skull which is now known as '' Eoanthropus,'' the '' Dawn Man.'' The age of the skull is measured in hundreds of thousands of years.

Fig. 63. On a building at '' The Hey '' poultry farm at Wivelsfield, Sussex, is this amusing weathervane of father and mother owls admonishing the baby owl. The owner of the farm was so tired of having constantly to grumble at his men because they rarely seemed to correctly note the direction that the wind was blowing from. As he wanted the chicken houses turned away from cold winds, he erected this vane to indicate to his employees the wind's direction.

Fig. 64. For more than 30 years this weathervane, showing a greyhound chasing a hare, has been turning in the wind on a building at the Homestall Kennels, Shovelstrode, Sussex, where the breeding of greyhounds is carried on. The breeding of greyhounds forms an important industry in this country.

Fig. 65. The patient and willing farm horse forms the subject of this weathervane on '' Pelling House,'' near Scaynes Hill, Sussex. The house was converted from what was an old barn on the farm.

Fig. 66. On a pole adjacent to some sheds where a '' rag and bone '' merchant stocked the objects he purchased, this ship-form of weathervane can be seen in Littlehampton, Sussex. As the cardinal points are missing it is possible the vane was a discarded one the merchant picked up.

Fig. 67. A blacksmith, Mr. Crowhurst, of Blindley Heath, Surrey, made this weathervane 50 years ago for the landlord of the local '' Blue Anchor Inn.'' The landlord, in those days, was a very keen follower of the foxhounds, and erected this vane on his building. The huntsmen and hounds still meet at the inn. The arrow shape under the fox shows that the fox faces the wind. The scroll work is similar to that in Fig. 61, Plate XXIV.

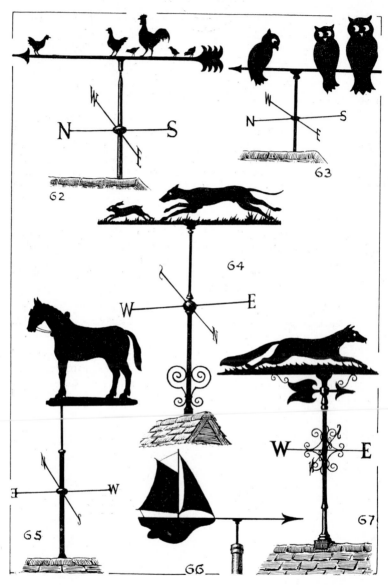

PLATE XXV

For notes on these vanes see p. 75

76

...hervanes on Private Dwellings

(*Introduction*)

The greatest number and variety of weathervanes are to be found on private dwellings.

Many owners or tenants of houses have weathervanes designed to express their own individual ideas. Some of the designs may not be of sufficient merit to satisfy the taste of artistic "highbrows," but they afford pleasure to the owner, and it is not often that one can be seen that is an "eyesore," and they certainly present a more picturesque "skyline" than the increasing number of television aerials, which are not beautiful. Occasionally weathervanes are made so that while they perform their primary function, the subject of the design is chosen to interest the junior members of the family, see Figs, 64, 68, 69, 72, 73, 74 and 78. Some tenants, having engineering ability, branch out and make their own weathervanes, see Figs. 65, 70, 74 and 78.

On a few houses the weathervane is designed to form a decorative finish to a cupola, gable, &c., as shown in Figs. 1, 2, 4, 5, 7, 9, 11, 20, 32, 66 and 67, while on others, on the ridge of the roof and elsewhere, the vane is an afterthought, erected because many tenants and members of their family find it useful as well as ornamental.

Gardening enthusiasts find weathervanes useful. Before lighting a bonfire they can ascertain the wind's direction and thus avoid having a fire on days when the smoke would be blown into their own or neighbour's house. The following old country saying reminds fishermen to study the wind's direction too.

> " When the wind is in the North
> The skilful fisher goes not forth ;
> When the wind is in the South
> It blows the bait in the fish's mouth."

People who have lived near a church and have been accustomed to glance at the church weathervane each morning to note the direction of the wind, so miss this habit when they move from the district that they find it necessary to erect a vane on their new dwelling. Before venturing out in Spring, Autumn or Winter, people knew it will be wise to don a thick coat should the vane show the wind to be coming from the East. The old saying : " When the wind's in the East, 'tis neither good for man nor beast," is a very true one.

PLATE XXVI

For notes on these vanes see pp. 79 *and* 80

78

Other old references to the wind's direction include :—" A Nor-wester is not long in debt to a Sou-wester," and, " Whatever wind prevails at 12 noon on June 21st, will prevail for the next three months."

A few private dwellings have weathervanes on the roof which record the direction of the wind on a dial on one of the interior walls (see Fig. 53, Plate XXXIII). Set in the overmantle of the King's gallery in Kensington Palace, London, is a map of Europe with one of the recording dials, while another recording dial over the fireplace can be seen at Longleat House, Warminster, Wiltshire. The dial at No. 1 Lewes Crescent, Brighton, is on the wall of the staircase.

The history of a weathervane on a private dwelling is often more difficult to trace than is the case of one on a public or business building, because tenants of houses move more frequently and invariably leave the vanes on the houses ; and since the vanes were put in position several tenants may have come and gone again.

Notes on Illustrations
of Weathervanes on Private Dwellings

PLATE XXVI

Fig. 1. Part of the fine old house named " Bedales," at Scaynes Hill, Sussex, was built in the 16th century. This banner-like weathervane, dated 1577, is on one of the gables. It has a pointer. It is not known when pointers came into use, probably not before the time of Charles I.

Fig. 2 is one of the many good vanes in the interesting old town of Abingdon, Berkshire, which is fortunate in having a society, " Friends of Abingdon," to help in preserving its old buildings. The vane illustrated is on Tompkins Almshouses, founded and endowed by the Tompkins family (wealthy Baptists), in 1731. Note the Tompkins initials and date, and absence of the cardinal points.

Fig. 3. This is another of Abingdon's good weathervanes and is on a house in " The Vineyard." The pointer is attractive in design and good style letters are used.

Fig. 4. This weathervane on a house in Ock Street, Abingdon, Berkshire, takes the form of an oak leaf. The cardinal points letters are larger than is usual, but are in a good Roman style and stand out clearly.

Fig. 5. Abingdon also possesses this weathervane. It is an early 18th century vane made by Abingdon craftsmen and it surmounts the cupola on the Long Alley Almshouses, built in 1466 by the Guild of the Holy Cross. This guild was dissolved under the Chantries Act, in 1553, and the Almshouses became Christ's Hospital under a master and board of governors. Now under the same management are the Twitty (built 1707) and the Brick Alley Almshouses (re-built 1718). The vane shows the stepped cross of the Guild of the Holy Cross, while R.E.6 refers to the granting of the Charter, by King Edward VI, to the new body in 1553.

Fig. 6. On the late 15th century moated Oxburgh Hall, Norfolk (home of the Bedingfield family for five centuries), was erected, in c. 1660, this lovely copper-gilt weathervane. The banner-like form, with beautiful and delicate pierced patterns, has in the centre, the arms of the Paston family. (Argents a chief indented or, six fleurs-di-lis azure, 3, 2, 1). When the vane was erected the Lady Bedingfield was the former Margaret Paston. This vane, minus a pointer, appears to be one of those whose primary purpose was to display the family arms. In 1952, Sybil Lady Bedingfield presented the building to the National Trust.

Fig. 7. In the 15th and 16th centuries, sculptured beasts, holding a rod with banner-like vane, were much used. The one illustrated (a griffin) is on the roof of the kitchen of the Manor House at Stanton Harcourt, Oxfordshire. The house, then a ruin, was pulled down in 1780, but the tower, gatehouse and kitchen remain. Medieval kitchen roofs had a louvre to allow smoke to escape. The opening of the louvre was regulated by the wind's direction, so a weathervane was a useful addition to the structure. "Hampton Court Accounts, A.D. 1535" give details of the construction of the louvre on the roof and mentions that it had round it twelve sculptured beasts all holding a rod and painted and gilded vane.

Fig. 8. Near West Grinstead, Sussex, is the remains of the Inner Tower or Keep of Knepp Castle, probably built about the time of William the Conqueror, as the Castle and Manor of Knepp, and forming part of the baronial possessions of William de Braose, who received them from the Conqueror in reward for his military services at the battle of Hastings. King John visited the castle in 1206 and 1215, using it as his hunting seat. It was destroyed in the Civil War. It is strange to see this weathercock, with its ragged tail and flag-like shape under it, rising from this ruined Norman tower. It is not known who put it there, or how long it has been in position, but an old print of 1835 shows the ruined tower with the weathercock on it. A short distance from the tower is a castellated residence built in the Gothic style by Sir Merrick Burrell, Bart., who inherited the old castle and land from his father. (A weathervane in the form of the family crest is shown in Fig. 9, Plate XVII).

PLATE XXVII.

Fig. 9. "Coolhurst," near Horsham, Sussex, built about 200 years ago, in the Tudor style, had the weathervane shown here on the house. It resembles the style of vanes used in the Tudor times (see Fig. 7, Plate XXVI). The residence was the property of Mr. Scrase-Dickens for some time. The family of Scrase originally came from Denmark and held land in Sussex before the Norman conquest. The principal part of the house was taken down and re-built. The stone beast, minus its rod and vane, now stands on a pedestal on the lawn near the house.

Fig. 10. This decorative banner-like weathervane is on the lodge at one of the entrances to "Paddockhurst," near Worth, Sussex. The design pierced on the vane represents part of the crest (a " demi-gryphon ") of the first Lord Cowdray. The mansion, a very find building, with lovely views stretching to the South Downs, belonged to the Cowdray family until recent years, when it was taken over by the Downside Abbey authorities, and now known as " Worth Priory," is used as a public school for 230 fortunate boys who have a fine old building and a glorious view to the South Downs in the distance. The stained glass windows in the music room contain a history of English music in pictures.

Fig. 11. On "Stratton House," Bath Street, Abingdon, Berkshire (one of three large Georgian houses built by the Tompkins family early in the 18th century), is this pennon-type weathervane which includes a small bird (believed by Mr. Greening Lamborn to be a " tom-tit " which would make a " punning coat ").

Fig. 12. In 1883, under the direction of Robert Whitehead (inventor of the torpedo), one of the additions was made to " Paddockhurst " (see No. 10), and this weathervane (pierced with the letter W), erected on it. The other addition to the mansion was erected by Westman Pearson (Lord Cowdray), in 1860 and this also has a pennon vane, with the monogram W P on it.

Fig. 13. It is strange to find this splendid " Kentish Horse " weathervane on the stables of an old Sussex House at Cuckfield, for none of the family of the owners are Kentish people, and the late Rev. H. F. Waller-Bridge (Vicar of the well-known Saxon church at Worth, Sussex, from 1917 to 1948), who lived in the house after his retirement, could give no information as to who erected the vane. His great grandfather gave a barrel-organ to Cuckfield Church, as stated on a tablet on the present organ. The arrow part of the vane clearly indicates the wind's direction as the horse is on its hind legs.

PLATE XXVII

For notes on these vanes see pp. 81 *and* 83

Fig. 14. While this decorative weathervane, over the garage at "Saxonbury," near Lewes, Sussex, provides a good surface area for the wind to act upon, its size rather overshadows the dainty scroll work on the four arms under it.

Fig. 15. The moated Maxstoke Castle, Coleshill, near Birmingham, is a splendid 14th century building that survived the Civil War without sustaining damage. It is a fine specimen of an Edwardian fortified manor house. The present owner is Mr. B. A. Fetherston-Dilke, and the weathervane displays the family badge. The lion is depicted in an alert position ready to face all comers. The vane, probably erected in Georgian times, is on the tower of the gatehouse in the East wall of the castle. (See the frontispiece). The castle was built in 1346 by Sir William de Clinton ; later it became the property of the Duke of Buckingham, and afterwards Queen Elizabeth conferred it on a Mr. Thomas Dilke, an ancestor of the present owner.

PLATE XXVIII

Fig. 16. Close to the church at Lindfield, Sussex, is a lovely gabled Tudor house in oak and mellowed red brick, with fine carved barge boards. Mr. C. E. Kempe, of stained glass fame, preserved and added to the building. This weathervane, on one of the additions to the house, shows the date 1888. The support is enriched with delicate scroll decoration. The house was the home of the Chaloners in the 16th and 17th centuries and was used as a workhouse in the 18th century. The letters have suffered in strong winds.

Fig. 17. No information is available as to the origin of this unusual weathervane on "The Boat House," Lyminster, near the Sussex coast. It was probably made by a boat-builder, for it is a fine model of a lifeboat. The tenant who erected it may have been a member of the lifeboat crew or a keen supporter.

Fig. 18. This very fine weathervane is unique. It is on a pole in the garden of "Eynsford Hill," Eynsford, Kent, the residence of the widow of the late Arthur Mee, who edited that splendid series of books *The King's England*. The vane was made by a Kentish craftsman (in Hyder's Smithy at Plaxtol), in copper, from a photograph of a silver model of Sir Francis Drake's ship, *The Golden Hind*, given to him by Queen Elizabeth. On the deck of the ship vane is a small treasure chest made of Roman lead, lined with Saxon oak, containing a bullet from the Spanish Armada, a fragment of stone from Drake's old home and an Elizabethan shilling which has touched Drake's Drum. The ship, with the good letters, is a beautiful example of a craftsman's work, a delight to look upon. The sails are so arranged that the pennants indicate the direction of the wind.

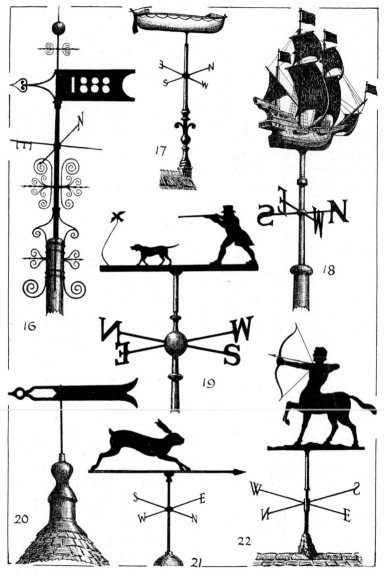

PLATE XXVIII

For notes on these vanes see pp. 83 *and* 85

Fig. 19. This weathervane, of an old sportsman shooting the flying bird, used to turn in the wind over an ironmonger's shop in Tonbridge, Kent ; but is now removed to another Kentish house. The bold letters indicate the cardinal points clearly. Note that the designer has remembered that a bird rising from the ground should fly into the wind.

Fig. 20. Dovecotes, of which this drawing shows the upper part of the conical roof and simple weathervane of one at Emping-ham, Rutland, were built by the lords of the manor to serve as homes for birds, which were used to provide extra meat for the table in winter time. The buildings were generally picturesque and provided hundreds of nests for the birds. The roofs formed suitable positions for weathervanes.

Fig. 21. An appropriate weathervane of a hare, is on the cupola of the barn belonging to Down House, Rottingdean, Sussex, where a pack of beagles used to be kept. Sir Edward Burne-Jones, the artist, lived in the village. He designed some lovely stained glass windows for the old church. William Morris carried out the work.

Fig. 22. A centaur (described in Greek mythology as a monster half man, half horse), about to shoot an arrow, forms this weathervane on " West Grinstead Lodge," Sussex. It was made by Messrs. Spooner & Gordon, Horsham, for a former owner of the house (Mr. V. Galsworthy, a cousin of the well-known novelist), as he was very keen on archery. Mr. Galsworthy may have seen the weathervane, erected about 1710, on the Guildhall at High Wycombe, Bucks., the design of which is similar.

PLATE XXIX

Fig. 23. As this vane is in the form of a raven it is very suitable to adorn a house called " Ravenshill," near Lingfield, Surrey. Note the letters G.D.T.K., which are used in place of the usual N.S.E.W. The tenant of the house in 1914, incensed at the Germans starting the war, had the vane made with the letters to represent " God damn the Kaiser." Perhaps he thought he was " doing his bit " in this way.

Fig. 24. Quite a number of Jewish people dwell in Brighton and Hove, Sussex, so it is not surprising to find this weathervane on the cupola of a house in King's Gardens, Hove. The design of the vane is a representation of Solomon's Seal, an old cabalistic Hebraic symbol, and was used as a talisman by Hebrews, and later by Christians. It is the traditional badge of Jewry and is now the emblem (two equilateral triangles crossed to form a pattern) of their flag.

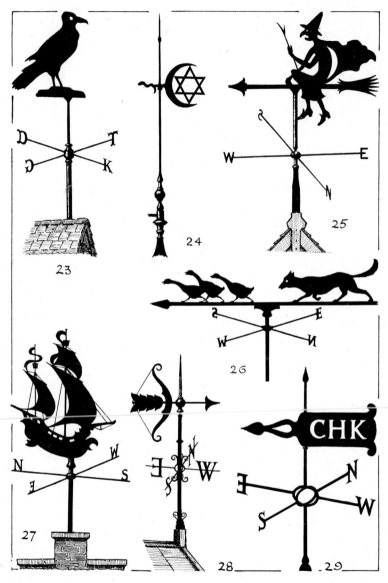

PLATE XXIX

For notes on these vanes see pp. 85 and 87

Fig. 25. This weathervane is on the gable of the garage at "Middle Lodge," Ardingly, Sussex, in the form of a witch on her broom, the end of the handle shaped like an arrow head for the pointer. The house is owned by a Lancashire family who brought the vane down South many years ago. In the 16th and 17th centuries, parts of Lancashire were supposed to be hot-beds of witches, and those found guilty of witchcraft were put to death.

Fig. 26. Over the stables of "Beech Hurst," a large house at Haywards Heath, Sussex, is this weathervane depicting a fox creeping up to pounce on the geese who are straining every nerve to escape. The vane is remarkable for the very fine live action seen in the animal and birds, and pays a tribute to the craftsman who made it.

Fig. 27. A design of a conventionalised form of ship, which, if not accurate in shape, is very decorative with its graceful and flowing curves. The bows of the ship point in the direction the wind is blowing from. The vane is on a house, "The Pantiles," Offingham Lane, Worthing, Sussex.

Fig. 28. The arrow-type of weathervane is fairly common, but this one of bow and arrow is most unusual. The very graceful form of the bow, and the Roman-type letters go to make this a most pleasing design. It is on a greenhouse attached to a mansion near Warninglid, Sussex.

Fig. 29. On a house near Lindfield, Sussex, is this nicely-shaped pennon-type weathervane having pierced letters (probably the initials of a former owner). Note the uncommon type of mounting (one oval crossing the other) used for the arms, having a good style of Roman letter to indicate the cardinal points.

PLATE XXX

Fig. 30. A Hailsham blacksmith, Mr. Crocker, made this weathervane for Mr. and Mrs. Green, of "Homecourt," a house in this Sussex town. The vane is similar to the one on Hailsham Church, except that it has the date and initials of the owners of the house. They were so pleased with the result of the smith's work that they asked him to include his initials at the bottom. This appreciation of good craftsmanship is most gratifying. The decorative support for the letters is pleasing in design.

Fig. 31. This model of the late Sir Henry Seagrave's *Golden Arrow* racing car forms the weathervane on a flagstaff in the garden of 15 King Henry Road, Lewes, Sussex. The model, painted in colours (the tail red, white and blue), was made by the late Mr. J. C. H. Martin, of Martin's Garage, Lewes. He was himself a very keen motor racing enthusiast.

PLATE XXX

For notes on these vanes see pp. 87 *and* 89

Fig. 32. From the windows of a house, "Domus," South Cliff Parade, Broadstairs, Kent, can daily be seen seagulls flying and gliding gracefully around, so it is not surprising that the owner of the house was attracted by this weathervane, a splendid gilded copper model of a seagull in flight. It is a pity that the letters and their supports are not up to the high standard of the gull above them.

Fig. 33. On the garage of "White Croft," Cooden Drive, Bexhill, Sussex, is this weathervane, the design representing "Pegasus," the winged horse, but it lacks the grace and action shown by the one in Fig. 7, Plate XI. The vane was made in 1936 for the owners by the "Sussex Ironworkers," Eastbourne.

Fig. 34. This beautifully made peacock weathervane, with its graceful lines and proportion, was found on the buildings of "Old Plaw Hatch," Sharpthorne, Sussex, by the present tenants when they took possession of the premises, and they have no information as to its age or who put it there. The peacock is a fine example of craftsmanship.

Fig. 35. The owner of the house, "West Riddens," Ansty, Cuckfield, Sussex, requiring a weathervane which would suggest his interest in his racehorses, commissioned Mr. Allen, a craftsman of Hurstpierpoint, to construct the vane shown by this drawing. The horse and jockey are in sheet metal, and the jockey's cap and garment are painted in the owner's colours.

Fig. 36. Taken down in 1949 for repairs, this weathervane of the flying geese was on a building at "Beech Hurst," Haywards Heath (see Fig. 26, Plate XXIX). The representation of flight is very skilfully portrayed by the craftsman who made the vane.

Fig. 37. Surely no weathervane similar to this can be found, which depicts an 18th century priest preaching to empty chairs. The late Sir Edwin Lutyens designed this vane for "The Deanery," a house at Sonning-on-Thames, Berkshire, and wrote across the design, "The unpopular priest—He ever speaks the truth, yet turns with every wind."

PLATE XXXI

Fig. 38. A lady, who was a previous tenant of the house, "Campden," Broad Street, Cuckfield, Sussex, and was interested in classical dancing, had this weathervane, of a delightfully graceful dancer, erected in 1937 on a flagstaff in the garden. The craftsman who made this fairy-like vane possessed a high degree of skill and appreciation of pleasing lines.

Fig. 39. Near Twineham, Sussex, on a house on the Henfield and Albourne Road, this weathervane, in sheet metal, showing a barque in full sail, swings in the wind, with its bow pointing to the

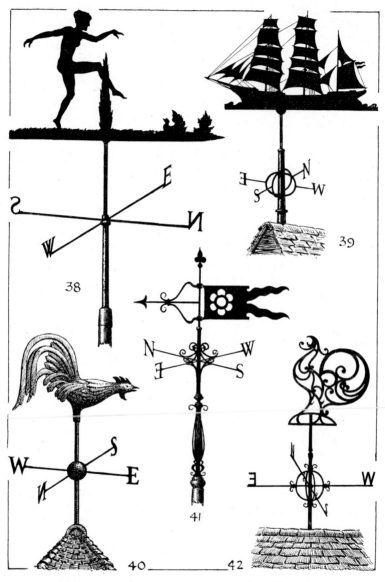

PLATE XXXI

For notes on these vanes see pp. 89 *and* 91

direction the wind is blowing from. The son of the owner of the house was a cadet on a barque sailing in Japanese waters when the 1939-1945 war broke out. He was made a prisoner by the Japs, and when he arrived home at the end of the war, he found this weathervane in position. His father had it made from a photograph of the ship, by Mr. Allen, of Hurstpierpoint, who has made several good vanes.

Fig. 40. This fine bronze weathercock, modelled in the round, with good-proportioned Roman-style letters, is on Dr. Hunter's house "Pelhurst," Rookery Way, Haywards Heath, Sussex. The weathercock was presented to the doctor on his retirement, by the grateful inhabitants of Wivelsfield.

Fig. 41. On the garage of "Littlefields," Pound Green, Buxted, Sussex, is this pennon-type weathervane, having been in this position for the last 20 years. The present owner purchased it when it was taken down from a nearby house that was undergoing structural alterations. It was, originally, on a house at Maresfield, Sussex. The pennon, with its wavy points and the iron scroll work make a graceful design.

Fig. 42. Although made 20 years ago, by Mr. Minihame, a Sussex blacksmith of Cowfield, it is doubtful if another weathercock similar to this can be found in this country. It is on the garage of "Spronketts," Bolney, Sussex, which was once a large farmhouse, but is now a private residence. The representation of a "crowing cock," full of graceful harmonising curves and scrolls of wrought iron, is a delightful specimen of craftsmanship which shows that the blacksmith possessed skill much above the average.

PLATE XXXII

Fig. 43. This arrow form of weathervane on the stables of a house in Hurstpierpoint, Sussex, differs from the one shown in Fig. 55, in that the space between the two ends of the arrow are decorated with a very delicate scroll design, and the end representing the feathers of the arrow is more decorative.

Fig. 44. It is rarely one sees a weathervane in the form of a pheasant in flight like this one which used to be on a flagstaff of a house near Pound Hill, Sussex. On the outside of one of the walls of this house is an interesting feature, four 15th century Persian tiles, modelled in low relief and having exquisite colouring. The owner of the house found the tiles, and not recognising their artistic value, had them cemented on the wall and the frost has cracked two of them.

Fig. 45. For obvious reasons the exact situation of the house on which this weathervane is erected is not given. As the drawing shows, the weathervane is in the form of a stork (painted in black and

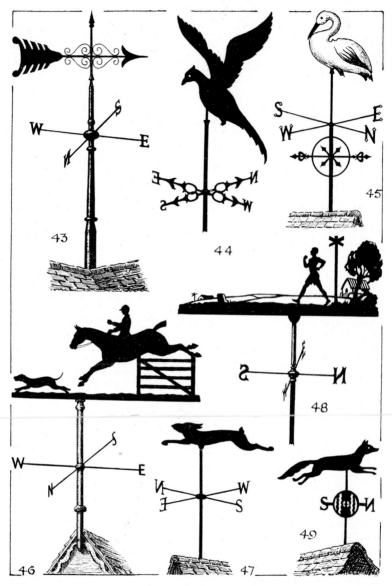

PLATE XXXII

For notes on these vanes see pp. 91 and 93

white) minus its legs. The vane is on a house in Sussex which is occupied by two bachelors. The stork appears to be solemnly meditating the position. The house contains many artistic treasures, one of which is unique, as it consists of a set of four very large electric light shades made from painted silk which once adorned the walls of the Palace at Pekin. The lovely Chinese decoration on these shades is very beautiful.

Fig. 46. The cottage on which this weathervane of a huntsman and foxhound is erected is on the Marquess of Abergavenny's estate at Eridge, Sussex, not far from Eridge Castle, the family residence, where a pack of foxhounds is kept, so the reason for the choice of this design for the vane is not difficult to understand.

Fig. 47. The most noticeable feature of this weathervane on the ridge of the roof of "Wayside," a house near Heathfield, Sussex, is the clever suggestion of the speed of the hare, although only two legs of the animal are shown.

Fig. 48. Those who, some years ago, took an interest in the annual Stock Exchange walking race from London to Brighton, will remember the late Mr. Hammond winning the race several times. When he retired he was presented, in 1929, with this unique weathervane showing him on his way to Brighton. Note the fine action of the walker and the clever suggestion of the Countryside with two signposts and milestone. Before Mr. Hammond's death the vane was on a mast at his residence at Haywards Heath, Sussex, but his widow moved it to her new home at "Langford," Burgess Hill, Sussex.

Fig. 49. Another fox weathervane in the countryside in which the Southdown Hunt operates, this one, differing from the four other vanes shown in this book which use a similar motif for the design. It is on a house, "Chevrons," near Clayton, at the foot of the South Downs, Sussex. Note the unusual mounting of the letters, which is similar to the vane shown in Fig. 49, Plate XXIII. It is possible that the same craftsman made both vanes.

PLATE XXXIII

Fig. 50. Still in the hunting district near the South Downs, the owner of this weathervane, showing huntsman and hounds, purchased it from an antique dealer and erected it on his house on the Albourne to Henfield road in Sussex. It is painted to represent the natural colourings. The grouping of the hounds is cleverly arranged and required much skill on the part of the craftsman who made it.

Fig. 51. On a pole in the garden of a house near Polegate, Sussex, this weathervane, depicting a wild duck in flight, swings in the wind. The wild birds on the nearby Pevensey marshes may have suggested the design of this vane.

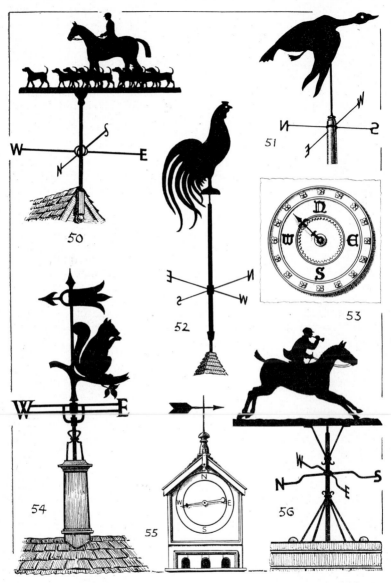

50

51

52

53

54

55

56

PLATE XXXIII

For notes on these vanes see pp. 93 *and* 95

Fig. 52. This very graceful weathercock on the roof of a summer house in a garden of a house named "Clockhouse," at Lindfield, Sussex, is quite different from all the other weathercocks illustrated in this book. The design represents a Silver Duckwing Yokohama cock. Note the lovely tail and small head of the bird. A former owner of the house used to breed these birds.

Fig. 53. Some weathervanes are connected to a moveable hand on a dial on an interior wall of a building. As the vane on the roof revolves in the wind, the hand on the dial shows the direction the wind is blowing from. This dial illustrates the one on the wall of the staircase at "Coolhurst," near Horsham, but the exterior vane is now missing.

Fig. 54. A house called "Timbers," situated in a lovely wooded district near Titsey, Surrey, has on its roof this elaborate weathervane depicting a squirrel eating his nut. A pennon shape vane with a pointer has been added to the top so that there would be no doubt as to the wind's direction. The mounting of the vane and the letters is uncommon and pleasing in design. The district in which the house is situated is an ideal one for squirrels.

Fig. 55. It is unusual to find a weatnervane recording dial on the exterior of a building as can be seen on an old dovecote on the roof of a building at Hovingham, Yorkshire. The hand is operated by gear wheels attached to the spindle of the vane.

Fig. 56. A former owner of the house named "Weathervanes," Dyke Road, Hove, Sussex, was a sporting gentleman and had this weathervane of a huntsman erected on his house, and another vane, depicting a foxhound in "full cry" on his garage. The vanes have been in position since 1935 when the owner changed the name of his house from "Elsinore" to the name of a racehorse "Weathervanes." The action of horse and rider is well portrayed.

PLATE XXXIV

Fig. 57. A house bearing the name of "The Friars," Rye Close, Worthing, Sussex, has this weathervane on its gable. The vane, showing three jolly friars tasting wine from the barrel standing between two of them, was obviously designed specially to represent the name of the house.

Fig. 58. This weathervane is unique in Sussex for it was made from an English design by a blacksmith in Sicily. It is on a gable of Mr. Milne's house, "Dykes," Henfield. The spirited action of the horse with its beautiful curves and very graceful tail is most pleasing. It is a pity that the letters are not so well formed.

57

58

59

GO

6I

PLATE XXXIV

For notes on these vanes see pp. 95 and 97

Fig. 59. This really fine design, modelled in copper, of a dragon in an aggressive mood, forms the weathervane on "Wynchdene," South Cliff Parade, Broadstairs, Kent. The graceful neck and tail and fine shaped wings are most pleasing in form, and display the high skill of designer and the metal worker who constructed it.

Fig. 60. Another "huntsman's" weathervane in the South Downs district of Sussex. This one is on the barn of the house named "Paternoster," on the Warninglid Road. The vane shows the return of the huntsman at the end of his day's sport. Note how cleverly the weariness of the hounds is expressed.

Fig. 61. This is one of those quaint and amusing weathervanes to be seen on some houses. The owner of this one purchased it at the agricultural show near Eastbourne in 1938 and erected it over the garage of his house at Shortbridge, near Pilt Down, Sussex. The vane was made by Spooner & Gordon of Horsham.

PLATE XXXV.

Fig. 62. Recently this weathervane, showing wild fowl rising from marshy grass, was erected on the rear premises of a house named "Boarsland," at Lindfield, Sussex, and forms an effective silhouette against the sky. The scroll supports for the letters are larger and longer than is usual.

Fig. 63. As part of a scheme to encourage Sussex decorative wrought-iron craftsmen, Lord Courthope ordered this very attractive weathervane to be made and erected on a gable of his house, "Whiligh," Sussex, about a quarter of a century ago. The actions of the horses and ploughman are cleverly portrayed. As the Estate is agricultural in character the design is most appropriate. Oak trees, hundreds of years old, from the park surrounding the house, supplied all the timber to repair the wonderful hammerbeam roof of Westminster Hall, London.

Fig. 64. The occupant of a house in Western Road, Haywards Heath, Sussex, made this weathervane, representing a French sailor, painted it in colours to display uniform and flag, and erected it on his garage. Although the vane hasn't a pointer, the flag shows the direction of the wind.

Fig. 65. A motor engineer, Mr. Awcock, who is a lover of dogs, constructed this weathervane and erected it on a flagstaff in his garden at 9 Milton Road, Haywards Heath, Sussex. The scroll design mounting of the arms, supporting the four letters, differs from any other vane illustrated in this book.

Fig. 66. Mr. Vickers, a very keen angler, had this weathervane of a pike made by a London firm of metal craftsmen for a building in the garden of his house, "Lucas," Lucastes Avenue, Haywards Heath, Sussex. The fish is a model of a pike constructed of copper.

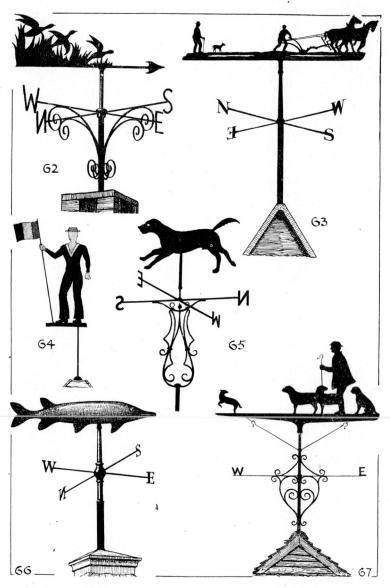

62

63

64

65

66

67

PLATE XXXV

For notes on these vanes see pp. 97 *and* 99

Fig. 67. This sheet metal weathervane, depicting a shepherd with his crook and dog, two sheep and frisky lamb, with some pleasing wrought-iron scroll work on the support, is on a house known as " Shepherds," Bolney, Sussex. The vane is another fine piece of work by the Cowfold blacksmith, Mr. Minihame, who also made the weathervane illustrated by Fig. 42 on Plate XXXI. A replica of this vane was taken by another client, to remind him of the lovely Sussex Downs and its famous sheep, to Ceylon.

PLATE XXXVI.

Two of the weathervanes illustrated on this plate (Figs. 68, 72) can be seen in several counties, and are stock designs of some firms of metal workers who keep them for clients to choose from when these people are not particular about the design, nor care whether other people have similar vanes on their houses.

Fig. 68. For more than 30 years this weathervane, depicting " Dick Turpin " holding up the vehicle and its occupants has been swinging in the wind. It is on a house in Jamison Road, Bexhill-on-Sea, Sussex. The action of men and horses is good but the wheels look none too strong to support the coach.

Fig. 69. The constructor of this quaint weathervane on " Pell House," near Wadhurst, Sussex, evidently possessed a sense of humour. The tenants of the house found it in position when they took possession. The vane may have been designed to amuse some children. Note the letters fixed at right-angles to the arms.

Fig. 70. This is another of the home-made weathervanes, designed and constructed by Mr. Church (who is interested in mechanical objects), and erected it on his garage in Sydney Road, Haywards Heath, Sussex. The dragon, with head turned facing its tail is picturesque. Mr. Church has also made another weathervane (an heraldic lion), incorporating an efficient anemometer.

Fig. 71. Several houses in South Cliff Parade, Broadstairs, Kent, have weathervanes. This one on " The Bungalow," depicts a conventional form of ship, constructed in copper. Note the pleasing form of the billowing sail at the stern and the very graceful shape of the pennant.

Fig. 72. The subject of this design is supposed to be " Mother Goose," and the vane is on " Brook Cottage," Slaugham, a small village in Sussex, in whose churchyard is the grave of the sister of the famous Horatio Nelson.

Fig. 73. A young lady with her umbrella blown " inside out " forms a quaint design for this weathervane. This one on the house known as " Red Cottage," Staplefield, Sussex. Note the dog leaning against the wind.

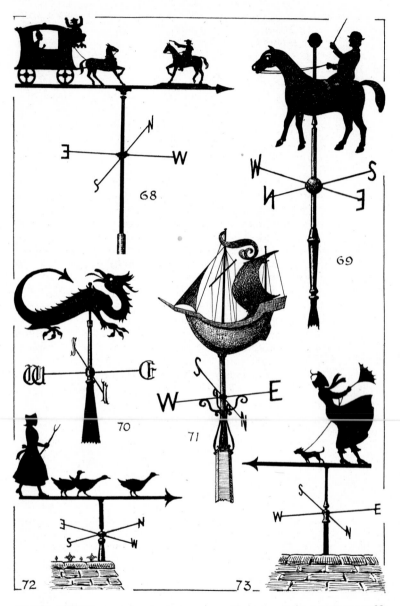

68

69

70

71

72 73

PLATE XXXVI

For notes on these vanes see p. 99

100

PLATE XXXVII

Fig. 74.   This is, as can be seen, a " home-made " weathervane without the cardinal points being indicated.   It is made of wood and metal and is coloured.   The vertical piece of wood, under the figure, is forced round by the wind until the four bladed propeller is square with the wind's direction, when it revolves.   By means of two crank wheels and connecting rod which turn with the propeller, the figure moves its arms and body, and thus appears, itself, to be turning the handle and propeller.   This vane is in a cottage garden near Cuckfield, Sussex.

Fig. 75.   On Muster House, Haywards Heath, Sussex, is this weathervane, the graceful form of a swallow in flight (painted with black and white).   The vane was designed by Miss Helena Hall of the nearby village of Lindfield.   The village plumber, Mr. Ede carried out the work.

Fig. 76.   This weathervane, made in 1946, is on a lantern form on top of the conical roof of an oast house (converted into a dwelling) named " The Round," near Buxted, Sussex.   A former tenant bore the name of Tuppin, and maybe his idea in choosing this design was a suggestion to display his name " T " up (above the building) " in " (the hand).

Fig. 77.   The owner of this weathervane has no connection with the sea.   He and his wife bought the vane at the market at Lewes, Sussex, because they liked it, and erected it on their premises near Chailey, Sussex.   The vane shows the vessel heading towards the buoy on which a wave is breaking.

Fig. 78.   Mr. Jenner, an engineer, made this weathervane, which has a ball-bearing, and erected it on a building in his garden in Lorne Road, Brighton, Sussex, to show the wind's direction and also to amuse his children.   The expressions on the face of the cat and the mouse are cleverly portrayed.

Fig. 79.   While this is not in the usual form of a weathervane, the arrow-type of vane on this cowl is operated by the wind's action to move the cowl's outlet away from the direction the wind is blowing from.   This cowl is one of the devices used to cure a smoking chimney, and is fairly common.

Fig. 80.   This quaint and amusing weathervane is a drawing from an old photograph supplied to the author by a friend, who was, unfortunately, unable to remember the house and district where the photograph was taken.   In spite of this, the vane is included here to show the contrast between this witch and the one illustrated by Fig. 25, Plate XXIX, and the clever representation of the cat.

Fig. 81.   A house, " Sunny Corner," close to the sea, in Cooden Drive, Bexhill, Sussex, has on its roof this ship in full sail. The proportions of ship and graceful lines of sails form a more pleasing weathervane design than No. 77.

74

75

76

77

78

79

80

81

PLATE XXXVII

For notes on these vanes see p. 101